Gift of Father Loughery OP

1945

LITURGY AND PERSONALITY

GOLDEN MEASURE BOOKS

The measure of the things of the spirit transcends the classification of any school. It has to do with genuine achievement in true liberty of spirit. The books which appear in the *Golden Measure* series will fall under very varied headings: history, works of the imagination, memoirs, essays on politics and esthetics, spiritual writings, philosophical and religious research; their authors may come from various countries and be of different spiritual families. The unity of the series will be due to its spirit — to a common respect for the image of God in man and in a common feeling for liberty. Such was the idea behind the collections published in France — the *Roseau d'Or* and *Les Iles*. It is our hope that the *Golden Measure Books* will form a part of the library of all those who love truth and beauty, who are anxious to understand the world and the problems of the present day, and who are solicitous of all that is bound up with the destiny of the human person.

Liturgy and Personality is the fourth volume in the new series to be edited for Longmans, Green and Co., by Jacques Maritain and Julie Kernan.

LITURGY AND PERSONALITY

BY

DIETRICH VON HILDEBRAND

LONGMANS, GREEN AND CO.

NEW YORK · TORONTO

1943

LONGMANS, GREEN AND CO.
55 FIFTH AVENUE, NEW YORK

LONGMANS, GREEN AND CO. LTD.
OF PATERNOSTER ROW
43 ALBERT DRIVE, LONDON, S.W. 19
17 CHITTARANJAN AVENUE, CALCUTTA
NICOL ROAD, BOMBAY
36A MOUNT ROAD, MADRAS

LONGMANS, GREEN AND CO.
215 VICTORIA STREET, TORONTO

LITURGY AND PERSONALITY

First .edition March 1943
Second edition October 1943

PRINTED IN THE UNITED STATES OF AMERICA

CONTENTS

The author wishes to acknowledge his debt to Dr. Emmanuel Chapman of Fordham University for his aid in editing and revising the English text of this book.

INTRODUCTION

Liturgy and Personality — that is, the spirit embodied in the Liturgy, the spiritual moulding of the man who lives in that spirit, and the personality thereby acquired — is one of the widest of themes; for it is the spirit of the God-Man who speaks to us in the Liturgy, and a full study of this theme includes both the development of personality and an analysis of the essence of the Liturgy and Personality. The present work will not attempt to treat this theme in its entirety. Only some of its basic aspects will be considered here, those aspects especially which more easily escape our attention. In some cases where they are obvious or have been dealt with adequately elsewhere, even very important features will be left to one side. These considerations may help the individual to assist in the celebration of the Liturgy with deeper awareness, keener insight into its inexhaustible depths, its classicism, its profoundly organic nature, and a new open-mindedness to its essential pre-eminence over all other forms of devotion. In regard to the Liturgy, more than to all

1

other forms of worship, may be proclaimed the words of Christ to the Samaritan woman: "If thou didst know the gift of God!"

1. — WHAT IS MEANT BY THE LITURGY

Opinions are divided as to the extent of the meaning of the word Liturgy. Some seek to apply it to all the divine services performed by a priest in the service of the Church, including May devotions, the Stations of the Cross and other special services, as well as the recitation of the Divine Office. Others restrict its scope to the Holy Mass, the Divine Office, and to the administration of the sacraments and sacramentals. We have no intention of taking part in this controversy, and we shall apply the word Liturgy to that which is indisputably defined as such and about which there is no difference of opinion — to the Holy Sacrifice of the Mass, which is Liturgy in the highest sense, to the Divine Office and to the administration of the sacraments and sacramentals.

2. — THE PURPOSE OF THIS BOOK

Although the present book seeks to stress the exceptional personality-building forces contained in the Liturgy, we must at the same time emphasize that the primary intention of the Liturgy is not to be sought in the formation of personality. The Divine Office is recited primarily because all praise and glorification is due to God, the fullness of all holiness and majesty, and not because it will bring about a transformation in ourselves. The Liturgy is not primarily intended as a means of sanctification or an ascetic exercise. Its primary intention is to praise and glorify God, to respond fittingly to Him. This intention is expressed in the words of the *Gloria* in the Holy Mass: "We praise thee, we bless thee, we adore thee, we glorify thee. We give thee thanks for thy great glory. . . For thou only art holy. . . Thou only art most high. . ." The same intention is expressed in the prayer *Sacrosanctae et individuae Trinitati* recited at the end of the Divine Office of the day.

The second intention is to ask for the grace of God, but even here the recitation of the Office must not be conceived as a psychological means of preparing the way for grace, as in the case of fasting, silence, discipline and other such practices considered in a purely ascetic sense. The intention of the

Breviary is not to improve our moral life by our own
power but to implore God to grant our religious petitions.   Both these intentions are discernible in the
Aperi, which precedes the recitation of the Office:
*Ut digne, attente ac devote hoc officium recitare
valeam, et exaudiri merear ante conspectum divinae
Majestatis tuae.*   (That I may pray to, and praise
Thee with attention and devotion, and may worthily
be heard before the presence of Thy Divine Majesty).   The primacy of the first intention of the
Liturgy, that of giving fitting praise to God, is distinctly expressed in the concluding words of the
prayer: *Domine, in unione illius divinae inten-
tionis, qua ipse in terris laudes Deo persolvisti, has
tibi horas persolvo.*   (Lord, in union with that Divine intention wherewith Thou didst Thyself praise
God while as Thou wast on earth, I offer these hours
unto Thee).

   To glorify God is also the primary intention of
the Holy Mass.   To this should be added the be-
stowal of redeeming grace upon men.   But Holy
Mass must never be celebrated with the sole intention of participating in its graces.   The intention of
adoring God and sacrificing to Him "through Christ,

with Christ, and in Christ," is the true condition for renewed incorporation in Christ and the amplification of grace.

Finally, man's participation in divine life is the primary purpose of the sacraments. In the reception of the sacraments the dominant intention is obviously sanctification and union with God, although the final aim of sanctification must be to glorify God. It is important to grasp that here too, as in the case of Holy Mass and the recitation of the Divine Office, to conceive of the sacraments as a psychological means for sanctification — as, for instance, ascetical exercises in themselves — would imply a radical failure to understand their true nature. Although a certain disposition of the person is necessary for the fruitful unfolding of the spiritual life, from the *volo* of baptism to the contrition required for a true and even valid confession, this effect nevertheless cannot be achieved through the disposition as such, but only through a gratuitous act of God, for which man's disposition is only a pre-condition.

Again, we must particularly stress that in examining the process of personal transformation brought about through the spirit incarnated in the Liturgy, we are not interpreting the Liturgy as any kind of pedagogical means.

To show that such a process of transformation exists does not mean that this is the essential aim of the Liturgy, or that it is the intention with which it is or can be carried out.   On the contrary, we shall see further that one of the special reasons for the strength and depth of the transformation of personality brought about by the Liturgy is that this transformation is not the end in view, and more than this, that the Liturgy is carried out with another intention entirely.   For the deepest transformation of personality occurs, not when means for this transformation are deliberately sought, but when it is brought about in an entirely gratuitous manner through an attitude meaningful in itself.   This attitude is like that of love which is entirely directed towards its object, a love which in its very essence is a pure response to value, which comes into existence only as a response to the value of the beloved, and which would cease to exist as soon as it became a pedagogical means for one's own improvement.   From such an attitude emanates a liberating, mellowing, value-disclosing action of incomparable strength and intensity.   And if Plato is right in saying that the soul grows wings as it beholds values, this act of beholding must be understood as an irradiation of the self by the Sun of Values, as a readiness to give oneself to, and to be immersed in, this radiation.   The soul grows wings — that is, the deepest inner transformation takes place — only if a real penetration of values and a real self-forgetfulness are reached. Were this act of "beholding values" to become a means of attaining such transformation, at that very moment it would cease to be a genuine irradiation by values, and they no longer would be taken in their proper seriousness; there would no longer be a true communion with the world of values, and the deep transformation would thus cease to operate.

The deepest *pedagogical* effect is achieved through that which is not used *as a pedagogical means:* it is achieved through that which, independent from pedagogical action, dispenses it as a *superfluum* or gift of super-abundance.   Thus the deepest and most organic transformation of man in the spirit of Christ is found precisely at that point where we purely respond to values, in the giving up of our-

selves to God's glory, in the glorifying of God performed as divine service, in the abiding *Coram ipso,*
(in standing before Him), in the rejoicing in God's
existence, in the *Gloria Domini,* (the glory of the
Lord), in the *magnalia Dei,* (the great deeds of the
Lord).   As we pray and sacrifice liturgically —
and this means through Christ, with Christ, and in
Christ — glorifying God, the spirit of Christ is im-
printed upon us, *Induere Christum,* as the Liturgy
proclaims.

But need we stress this action and invest it with
a conscious meaning, since it comes about of itself,
and even more, must not be aimed at for itself?
Yes, for in the first place the examination of the fundamental attitudes created by the Liturgy means a
deeper understanding of the Liturgy and its spirit,
and enables us to perform it more consciously and
genuinely.   And more than this, the Face of Christ
is revealed in the Liturgy: it is Christ praying.   To
learn the fundamental dispositions embodied in the
Liturgy means to penetrate more deeply into the
great mystery of the adoration of God, which is
Jesus Christ.   The more consciously the spirit of

Christ is grasped and realized in the Liturgy, the more the latter becomes for us a "way of following" Christ, the deeper the transformation of man in Christ.

Moreover, today we are in urgent need of such a study, for there are many who still prefer other forms of devotion and religious exercises. They do not recognize the fact that it is precisely the Liturgy which grants us the deepest and most organic form of development of the divine life received by us in baptism, and that the man who is entirely formed by the spirit of the Liturgy is like to Christ. Not that this formation is always achieved through the Liturgy. God is able to raise up out of stones children to Abraham. He may give this spirit to a man who has but scant familiarity with the Liturgy and prays little according to the forms of the Liturgy. But in each saint, reflecting the image of Christ in a new light, the spirit of the Liturgy lives not necessarily in his teachings nor in the forms of devotion introduced by him, but in his sanctity, in the fact of being a saint. It still remains true that the Liturgy, in its organic relation to inner prayer and asceticism, is the God-given path for growth in Christ. Those who do not perceive this fact should be reminded of the words already quoted: "If thou didst know the gift of God!"

I

THE LITURGY AND THE VOCATION
OF MAN

The meaning of all creation is to imitate and glorify God, the inconceivably glorious and holy. That which is created — whether it belongs to the reign of pure matter, as the sea or the mountains; or to the realm of organic life, as the plant and animal; or to the sphere of spiritual things, as a work of art, a cultural epoch, a community, or the spiritual person itself — exists only in order to imitate and glorify God inasmuch as it fulfills the divine idea in its regard and simultaneously unfolds the fullness of values to which it is ordained. For all values — goodness, beauty, the mystery of life, the noble light of truth, and even the dignity of being as such, as opposed to nothingness — all these are rays which radiate from God's being, Who is all holiness. Whatever is good and beautiful, all that possesses a value, is a reflection of His eternal light and imitates God according to its own fashion.

All these values are not only like a dew falling
from heaven but also an incense rising to God.   For
by this very token to be a value is to be a glorification
of God.   Whatever is praises God through that inner
preciousness which marks it as having been drawn
out of the indifferent.   Nature praises God in its
beauty not only because it speaks of God to man and
inspires him to praise God, but also in the silent
praise rising from its own beauty.   This is true of
every work of art, every perfect community, every
truth, every moral attitude.   Man, the most precious
creature known to us through experience, who is not
only a *vestigium* (trace) of God, but also an *imago*
(image) of God, is called not only through his value
to be an objective praise of God, like all the rest of
creation, but also to a consciously accomplished
glorification.

Man alone can make a conscious response to God's
endless glory.   He must first of all respond to each
value as a reflection of God with joy in that which
has a value, with enthusiasm, respect, love; and
above all he must adoringly love and lovingly adore
God, who is the fullness of all values.   For this
glorification of God voiced in loving adoration rep-

resents quite a new dimension of glorification, a different degree of reality, as new as the personal being of the Subject being awakened and penetrated with lucid consciousness, and radically different from that of all impersonal being. The ultimate dignity of man consists precisely in that he can consciously adore and glorify God. But this conscious response to God's glory, in which the ultimate significance of man partly consists, does not stand juxtaposed to his vocation to praise God through his own value (and ultimately through his saintliness), but is closely linked with it. In man, the central personal values do not take shape "from themselves," as do his physical stature or his temperament; they grow, on the contrary, out of man's conscious communion with the world of values, out of his intentional turning to the realm of values, out of his act of giving himself up to God through his affirmation of values and his response to them. A person can never be good, if he does not desire the good, rejoice in it and love it. He cannot attain sanctification without adoring God, without loving Christ and bending his knee before Him.

Thus, the illumination received from the world of

values and from the Face of Christ, and the conscious response to God's glory, are the conditions
for man's inner transformation, the ripening of the
central personal values, and above all, of the supernatural beauty by which God is objectively praised
and glorified.   Conversely this "word" of praise is
the more adequate and authentic, according to the
degree that man is more perfect.   The vocation to
adore God and to glorify Him through conscious
acts can be fulfilled by man only to the degree that all
the central values are realized in him, and above all
to the degree that he resembles Christ, that is to say
is saintly.   Thus, the two currents of praise and
glorification — the objective silent one, expressed
through values, and the personally performed, conscious adoration — must not be divided in man:
they mutually condition each other, and the growth
of the one means the increase of the other.

The conscious glorification of God is also twofold
in character.   Not only do we owe God adoring
love expressed, on the one hand, in the affirmation of
all values and, on the other, in the immediate love of
God; we also owe Him *spoken* praise, an uttered act
of glorification.   Inasmuch as we are spiritual per-

sons, we are capable of a clearly formulated praise, of referring ourselves expressly to glorification, of an uttered "word" of praise. This uttered praise is organically linked to adoring love, but it brings something new in relation to the latter. According to the words of St. Augustine this expressed glorification will also resound in Eternity: *Vacabimus et videbimus, videbimus et amabimus, amabimus et laudabimus, quod erit in fine sine fine.* (We shall repose and we shall see, we shall see and we shall love, we shall love and we shall praise, what will be at the end without end).

The *Laudare* of the Sanctus, in which we join in the chant of the angels, is something apart from *amare,* to love. To be sure it flows forth out of adoring love, for the *amare* is the very soul of praise; but the expressed act of praise, lauding and glorifying, speaks yet in another way of the glory of God: it is the continuing act of adoring love, a confirmation and fulfillment of the latter. While the specific glorification of God is contained more implicitly in adoring love, and the latter is more like an ultimate and suitable response to God's endless glory and holiness — the act of praising, lauding and thanksgiving is an expressed gesture of glorification, a personal realization of that very gesture which is objectively conveyed through values.

This expressed glorification of God is also correlated with the objective glorifying of God through saintliness. The saint alone is capable of *authentically* praising God. As the twenty-third Psalm puts it: "Who shall ascend into the mountain of the Lord: or who shall stand in His holy place? The innocent in hands, and clean of heart." But then, it is through glorification, praise and sacrifice, that man is deeply transformed and sanctified. These two forms of glorification cannot therefore be separated. Of course, there exists a certain order of succession, as expressed in the words of St. Augustine: *Vacabimus et videbimus, videbimus et amabimus, amabimus et laudabimus, quod erit in fine sine fine.* Sanctification and adoring love go hand in hand, and the specific *Laudare* and *Glorificare* are organically linked to both of them. *Cantare amantis est* (to sing is the act of the lover), St. Augustine also says. But this order of succession in spiritual formation does not mean a succession in time of these forms of divine glorification. We shall better grasp the truth that the sanctification of man is entirely impossible without the *laudare* and *glorificare dominum,* after the following basic fact is examined.

Only the God-man, Jesus Christ, can truly offer adoration and love to God. He alone is entirely holy, He alone truly glorifies God through His holiness, and He alone can truly praise and laud God. The final, supernatural vocation of every man is, therefore, transformation into Christ. Only from Christ, with Him and in Him can we offer true adoring love to God and laud Him; and we can become holy only inasmuch as we cease to live, and Christ lives in us; that is to say, that the divine life implanted in us in baptism is fully developed. Our transformation into Christ is the essence of sanctity. This transformation of man into Christ includes not only the loving adoration of the Father with Christ and in Christ, but also the participation in the fulfillment of the sacrifice of Christ and the uttering of the "word," the only true laud and glorification, offered by Christ to His Heavenly Father. Even now, in spite of our imperfection and infirmity, we are permitted to join in the praise of the angels, because

as members of the mystical body of Christ, we pray
with the Head.   And the more fully we participate
in this expressed glorification of the Father in the
Laudare, the more we shall be transformed into
Christ.   Yes, we grow in the adoring love of Christ
for the Father to the extent that we participate in the
fulfillment of the *Laudare* and *Glorificare,* the exalted fruit of His adoring love.

Of course, this does not suffice for the transformation into Christ.   Apart from the indispensable foundations, participation in divine life
through baptism and its renewal and confirmation
through the sacraments, there is the loving immersion in Christ, living and doing according to the
spirit of Christ, following His teaching, following
Christ by carrying His cross, loving one's neighbor
with Christ.   All ascetic practices, all the "daily
work" of self-mortification, serve only this one purpose.   But one of the essential factors leading to
transformation into Christ is participation in the uttered glorification of the Father, and this glorification takes place especially in the Liturgy.   It leads
us into the secrets of the love of the God-man for the
Father and His glorification of the Heavenly Father,

and the love of the Heavenly Father for mankind. The conscious, fully awakened act of performing the Liturgy, seals into the soul the Face of Christ. In taking part in the Liturgy, we make our own the fundamental attitudes embodied in it.

It is with this process of transformation that the present book deals. Herein will be expounded the imitation of Christ which is organically achieved through participation in the Liturgy, though it should be remembered that the Liturgy is not performed for that express purpose. In other words, this work will deal with the expressly uttered *Laudare* and *Glorificare*, the third form of the glorification of God previously described as one of the three specific vocations of man in relation to the two other forms of glorification, adoring love and sanctification. It will deal with the *Laudare* and *Glorificare* with Christ and through Christ in the performing of the Liturgy. But, as we have already said, only a part of this theme will be dealt with here. We shall not speak of the relation of the spirit embodied in the Liturgy to sanctity as a whole, but only of certain elements of sanctification, which are less familiar to us, because they are not explicitly mentioned in the

commandments of God and in the demands emphasized by Catholic ethics.   The most important and
central elements will be intentionally excluded, as
for instance, how man, formed by the spirit of the
Liturgy, grows into the love of Christ, how our humility unfolds by participation in the Liturgy, and
so on.

The formative power of the Liturgy in constitut-
ing personality will be especially considered here;
this means the constitutive elements indispensable
for sanctification, and not the central point with
which the Sermon on the Mount deals.   This restriction is made in order not to repeat what has already
been said.   But this restriction, which obliges us to
limit ourselves to the personality-forming power, in
the narrower sense of the word, has nothing whatever
to do with the aesthetic overrating of that which is
commonly called "personality."   We are as far removed as possible from the "cult of personality"
which places above the simple fact of humbly obey-
ing God's commandments the question of whether or
not a man is a "full personality."   "Only one thing
is necessary": the glorification of the Father through
the imitation of Christ and participation in His glori-

fication. This however implies being a personality
in its true sense; that is, the saint alone is the true
and complete man, the true personality. Thus our
present study forms but a part of that other great
theme: "Be you therefore perfect, as also your heavenly Father is perfect."

II

THE ESSENCE OF PERSONALITY

In speaking of personality as distinct from the person, we have in mind something clearly defined. Every man is a person, in essence a conscious being, a subject, who enters into relations with others, who knows wills and loves. A person is a being who "possesses himself," who does not simply exist but who actively achieves his being, and has the power to choose freely. But every man is not a personality. Only persons can be personalities, but in order to be a personality it is not enough just to be a person. When is a man a personality?

The average man, the inoffensive, colorless, ordinary man without a clearly expressed individuality is not a personality. But neither is the abnormal man, the crank who astonishes others because of his peculiarities and falls out of the common range because of his oddities and eccentricities. Nor can the pathological man be considered a personality. A personality in the true sense of the word is the man who rises above the average only because he fully realises the *classical human* attitudes, because he knows more deeply and originally than the average man, loves more profoundly and essentially, wills more clearly and correctly than the others, makes full use of his freedom; in a word — it is the complete, profound, true man.

To confuse the "normal" man and the "average" man is an error typical of the narrow-minded Philistine. This error holds that the ordinary, average, run-of-the-mill type is the normal man, and that the one who differs from the average is the abnormal man, regardless of whether he is above or below the common range. The genius and the insane man seem related because both of them stand outside the range of the average man. But statistics do not decide what the normal man is, as the most numerous type of man is not the normal. The normal is that which most closely corresponds to the essence of man. A man is a personality who most fully develops this essence, who realizes entirely all the essential personal values. "Personality" is a mark of the normal man because in him the specifically personal is most fully and originally developed.

The average man is not the normal man; he is a spiritually immature and crippled man. Likewise, the fullness of personality which goes beyond the average is hardly related to the abnormal or psychopathic. It may even be said that the average man, the common type in whom the classical human attitudes are not fully expressed and freely developed, almost generally manifests abnormal traits — inhibitions, infantilisms, repressions.

Neither, of course, should the normal man be confused with the man who possesses all gifts and talents. The truly normal is the classical man who is fully capable of perceiving values and responding to them, the free, objective man, unrepressed and uninhibited, in whom the capacity for sacrifice and love is unbroken. There are men who are filled with so deep a thirst for happiness that harmless little joys cannot satisfy them, who stand in a direct elementary relation to being not rendered insipid and commonplace by conventions — men like Saint Augustine and Saint Francis even before their conversions. On the other hand, special gifts, philosophic and artistic genius for instance, gifts such as those possessed by a Michelangelo, Beethoven,

Goethe, are gifts of God which do not belong as such
to the normal man in the strict sense of the word.
They are *exceptional* gifts, not only because they
are rarely bestowed — normal men are also rare
— but because they represent special powers which
are not indispensable to man's essence in general
and his vocation; they are special values and gifts
which only certain men receive from God.   Every
normal man, in our sense of the word, is a personality, but this does not mean that he is a genius.   Under the term personality we understand
the complete, classical man, in whom are revealed
the great fundamental traits of man, undeviated and
unbroken.

Two essential components of personality must
here be distinguished: In the first place, the fullness of the essential spiritual "organ," the faculty of
love and knowledge, the power of will, the natural
potential of the person, the energy of life which flows
in it, we might say its "essential endowment," distinct from special talents; in the second place, the
organic link with the world of values and of truth,
perceiving them, abandoning oneself to them, living
in truth, in tune with the objective Logos, the absence

of all subjective deviations from the meaning of being. Each of these two elements taken separately is not sufficient for the constitution of personality. The first is a pure gift which we receive and to which we can add nothing, just as we cannot add a cubit to our physical stature. The second is, on the contrary, accessible to the influence of our will.

Usually, the question as to whether or not a man is a personality is inadequately concerned only with the presence of the first element. In the cult of personality inspired by a Napoleon, a Goethe, and many others, we are so carried away by the scale of this component that we do not notice those points which reveal a certain emptiness and lack of substance, a limitation and "impotence"; those points at which these men deviate from the objective logos of being because they have not been rooted in the genuine world of God from which they might draw true life. On the other hand, it is true that a man who has received a humble and limited "essential endowment" may by the best intentions and by service and sacrifice to the world of values, cease to be an average man, though he does not possess the scope, power and fullness of true personality. For the formation of personality both components must exist, not only side by side, but organically linked together.

A further distinctive trait of personality is that the entire being possesses unity of *style*. Its external being must not be inorganically and outwardly stamped on the inner being, but should be a genuine projection of the latter. By this is meant that rare harmony between the inner and the outer which one sometimes finds in men whose speech, expression, movements, external style of life, are organically moulded by their inner attitudes. Such men radiate a noble and powerful atmosphere; they are not dragged down to a lower level by the accidental conditions of their environment.

The power of emanating an atmosphere is not in itself, however, a sign of true personality. A man may also powerfully radiate a vulgar, trivial, common, and vain atmosphere. In such a case, he is not a personality in the true sense of the word designating a genuine and exalted value. The unity of style should be the expression of the true, authentic atmosphere of a life rooted in the metaphysical situation of man, of an attitude open to value and responding to value, and saturated by the super-natural world.

After what has been said, it is not further neces-sary to try to prove that the word personality is used incorrectly and inadequately when it is applied to men who possess a strong character, who assert them-selves and occupy a certain "space" because of their temperament. The power of self-assertion, whether expressed in a stream of irresistible vitality or strong formal energy and a keen sense of the aim pursued, is not sufficient to achieve personality in the deeper sense of the word. Neither can the individuality of certain persons be absolutely considered as person-ality, those qualities which cause us to define them as leaders, a certain conquering fullness and spirit-ual energy, which make them central figures around whom other human beings rally and crystallize in order to form a community. This power only rep-resents the first component of personality, the full, natural "essential endowment," whose existence does not in any way imply the presence of the second indispensable component. Its lack does not mean a lack of personality. There are quiet personali-ties, emanating only secret, hidden radiations.

A further question is whether it is possible for
every man to become a personality. Is not the full
capacity of perceiving values and the unbroken
power of responding to them, the fullness and
breadth of a man, conditioned by his talents? Are
there not insignificant men, stupid, ungifted, limited,
who with the best of intentions cannot demand for
themselves the fullness, breadth and freedom which
belong to true personality? And what of inwardly
insecure, unstable people who let themselves be over-
thrown by every breath of spiritual wind, brushed
aside by the least pressure? What of those who in
a new, impressive environment feel the ground slipping from under their feet, who are hopelessly carried away by the stream of public opinion, by the
fashionable or sensational? Are they not gregari-
ous men, average men, the very opposite of personalities?

Yes, considered from the purely natural point of
view. From the point of view of Goethe, for instance, there exist two categories of men: men who
are middling or possess at best a modest "essential
endowment," and *"personalities."* According to
this, it would be absurd to expect a middling man to

become a personality, just as it would be absurd to expect a man not musically gifted to become a Mozart.

But everything is different because of the inconceivable exaltation of humanity through the incarnation of God, because of baptism which implants in man a new principle of life, participation in the life of Christ and the Holy Trinity.   In so far as every baptized person develops this life in himself, and, even better, lets this life be developed in him, inasmuch as he gives himself up to Christ and follows Christ, living from Christ, with Christ and in Christ, he lives no more but Christ lives in him: he thus participates in the unlimited breadth and fullness of Christ.   He who is baptized in the life of Christ, he in whom Christ is truly imitated, the saint, becomes a personality, no matter what his "essential endowments" are.   Of course, grace does not replace but fulfills nature.   If an intellectually ungifted man attains sainthood, he does not suddenly acquire a philosophical and theological genius. Among saints, too, we find the same differences as between geniuses and plain, simple, not specially gifted men.   But the lack of gifts and the modest natural structure are no longer something depressing, narrowing and limiting because they have been transformed into that moving simplicity which is penetrated with the supreme wisdom of Jesus Christ; because the question of intellectual "significance" is surpassed through the participation in the unutterable breadth of God, in the pulsations of the most Sacred Heart, in whom are all the treasures of wisdom and knowledge, *in quo sunt omnes thesauri sapientiae et scientiae.*

Even if a man has received only a humble "essential endowment," which does not permit him to become a natural "personality," he is strong in his weakness if he fully develops the supernatural life received in baptism, that is, the new principle of life, new "organs" and powers. The saint, therefore, shows forth the two components of personality in a far higher sense: the supernatural "essential endowment," and the complete organic link with the world of supernatural values, holiness, the mysterious glory of God, which has revealed itself in the image of Christ, in whom all ties with the natural world of values are "surpassed" *per eminentiam.*

To speak of Saint John Vianney, the Curé of Ars,

of Blessed Brother Conrad or Blessed Brother Juni-
per as insignificant persons — even to raise such a
question — is to show a complete lack of understanding of the world of the supernatural.   The person of every saint — and this means one who no
longer lives himself but in whom Christ lives —
breathes a fullness, a breadth and height, whose
brightness surpasses even all the fullness and greatness of purely natural genius.   There is a deeper antithesis between the most simple, naturally humble,
gifted saint, as for instance John Vianney of Ars
and the petty limitations of the average man than between the rich intellectual world of a Goethe and the
latter; it is far more classical, more universal, more
illuminating; in it the breath of truth is felt in an
incomparably higher degree.   This does not mean
that saints receive analogous natural talents through
saintliness, but that they receive this light and fullness in Christ *per eminentiam*.

   To die to ourselves in order that Christ may live
in us, is thus the only path leading to full personality in a far truer and higher sense of the word; and
it is this path which is open through the grace of God
even to those who possess only a humble natural "es-

sential endowment." This dying to oneself, does not, however, mean the giving up of individuality. On the contrary, the more a man becomes "another Christ," the more he realizes the original unduplicable design of God which this man represents. Of course, this is only possible because Christ is the "Son of Man," because the whole of humanity is contained in Him, and above all, because not only is he man, but "the entire fullness of the Godhead lives in His Heart," *in quo est omnis plenitudo divinitatis.* Every imitation of man, even of the greatest, richest, most gifted man, even of a genius, would mean the giving up of one's individuality, a levelling, a renunciation of personality, not to mention the fact that an absolute, literal imitation of any man is entirely impossible. Therefore the unique inimitable design of God is fully and ultimately incarnated in a man only when he attains saintliness. Can one find more powerful, more deeply expressed individualities than Saint Catherine of Siena, Saint Francis of Assisi, Saint Augustine, Saint Paul, Saint Gregory VII?

Nevertheless it should be held in mind that it would be a great mistake to place before ourselves

the aim of becoming personalities in this higher
sense of the word, or of becoming powerful individualities.   However high the value attached to the
participation in the breadth and fullness of God, the
words of Christ can be applied to it: "Seek ye first
the kingdom of God and his justice, and all these
things shall be added unto you."

III

GENERAL CONSIDERATIONS OF THE INFLUENCE OF THE LITURGY ON PERSONALITY

As the preceding chapter has already indicated, a distinction must be made between the two fundamental elements in the formation of personality and its development in general. The first is the purely ontological basis for the development of personal life, which man can in no way bestow upon himself, a pure gift from the hand of God and from which man's freedom is excluded. This *natural* basis is the existence of man as a spiritual person, the presence of spiritual "organs" such as the powers of knowing, willing, loving, and the like. To these should be added the natural tendencies received by man through heredity. The *supernatural* basis of the imitation of Christ is the divine life implanted by baptism, which in us is partly restored and partly fortified through the sacraments. In this life making us members of the Mystical Body of Christ which is not only a moral but a mysterious physical link with Christ, bestowed as a pure gift of God, is found the ontological basis for the transformation into Christ, the vital principle of all saintliness.   To be endowed with this supernatural life, presupposes the existence of the natural ontological basis, that is to say, the essence of the person.   Such a supernatural life could never be granted to a material object or a material creature such as a plant or an animal.

The second, no less indispensable and fundamental element of all natural and supernatural formation of personality, is the intentional contact with the world of values.   We have already seen that natural moral values do not arise of themselves, as for example temperament or physical beauty.   They can only grow through the apprehension and affirmation of values, through a conscious response to them. The simple faculties of knowing, willing and loving do not as yet imply virtues; these spiritual "organs" do not confer humility, purity, love.   Virtues only blossom out of the conscious union of man with the world of values.   It is the same in regard to the supernatural life of man.   This fundamental element of intention in spiritual growth is not excluded from the supernatural realm, and for adult man, this conscious turning to God is demanded even for membership in the Mystical Body of Christ, as is shown in the *volo* (I will) of the baptismal rite, as well as in the existence of the baptism of desire and the baptism of blood. *Qui fecit te sine te, non te justificat sine te,* ("Who made you without you, will not justify you without you") says St. Augustine, and what is true of justification is also true of sanctification. Without the knowledge of Christ and of God revealed in Christ's visage, without the love of Christ, the epiphany of the invisible Father, without the following of Christ, no one can be sanctified: "I am the way, and the truth, and the life," says the Lord, and, "he who beholdeth me, beholdeth also the Father."

Without the ultimate free "yes" of dedication to Christ the God-Man, without a total giving of self to Christ, without the taking up of His cross, without the following of the essential commandment "on which dependeth the whole law and the prophets," the divine life implanted in us through baptism cannot reach its full development in us: "If any one love me, he will keep my word. And my Father will live in him, and we will come to him and will make our abode with him."

The meaning of the Liturgy for the formation of personality will be considered here from the point of view only of the second fundamental element, the *intentional* root of sanctity, and not from the point of view of the ontological influence. This purely ontological basis will be taken for granted, and therefore more stress will be put naturally on the Holy Mass and on the Divine Office than on the sacraments in which the ontological causality stands foremost.

When we examine the spirit embodied in the Liturgy and impressed upon the person through participation in the Liturgy, it appears that this spirit is revealed in three ways.

First of all, the spirit of the Liturgy is expressed in the liturgical act as such, in the Holy Sacrifice of the Mass, the eternal loving sacrifice of Christ; in the sacraments, the communicating love of Christ; and in the Divine Office, the loving adoration and eternal praise which Christ offers to His Heavenly Father.

In the second place, the spirit of the Liturgy expresses itself in the meaning and atmosphere conveyed by single prayers, antiphons, hymns, and the like, in all that the Liturgy expressly *says,* in the thought and spiritual climate which pervade its forms and words.

In the third place, the spirit of the Liturgy is expressed in its structure and construction; in the building up of the Mass, of the rites, of the different sacraments, of the Divine Office, in the alternate accentuation of praise, thanksgiving and prayer, in the structure of the liturgical year, in the rules according to which, for example, one feast takes precedence over another.

We shall attempt to examine certain fundamental features of the homogeneous spirit which is expressed in these three sources, and to show that these fundamental features are indispensable to the formation of a true personality.

We are not interested in historical questions regarding the epoch to which this or that part of the Liturgy belongs; what motives inspired their introduction into the Liturgy; whether they are of Roman, Gallic or Oriental origin. We are interested in the mysterious, all-embracing, qualitatively expressed unity of this spirit of the Church, of Christ who con-

tinues thus to live among us, of the Liturgy as the
voice of the Church, for the building of which ma-
terials were collected in all the different cultures
and epochs; a unity which is not broken, even when
the reasons which prompted the introduction of
this or that element are secondary and fortuitous.
Though an historical analysis carried out in its own
place and time may prove fruitful and be justified,
there is no room for it in our study.   We are not
interested in the formation of ancient or medieval,
Roman or Oriental man, but in the formation of the
supernatural personality in us, the formation of
Christ in us, as it has taken place in every saint,
not in his words and teachings, not in the form of
asceticism he has chosen, but in his saintliness, in
a Saint Augustine as well as a Saint Theresa of the
Child Jesus, in a Saint Francis as well as in a Saint
Bernard or a Saint Vincent de Paul.

IV

THE SPIRIT OF COMMUNION IN THE LITURGY

One of the deepest marks of the Liturgy is its character of communion-prayer. In the Holy Mass and in the Divine Office not only does the *We* dominate the *I*, but even when the *I* is uttered, as in the *Deus, in adiutorium meum intende,* or in the *Confiteor,* or in the *Domine, non sum dignus,* or in the Psalms, this *I* is completely built into the communion. It is uttered as issuing from the ultimate union of all in Christ, which precludes the omission or exception of other members of the Mystical Body. The Liturgy, as the official prayer of the Church, the prayer of the mystical Christ, is in its very meaning and essence the prayer of a community; each man, even when praying alone, enters consciously, if he understands this prayer, into the wider stream of prayer; he takes part in the prayer of the Head and through Him also of the Mystical Body of Christ. This distinguishes the Liturgy from the other forms of prayer and devotion, as for instance the holy rosary, the Stations of the Cross, the May devotions, or ordinary private prayer. Of course, even such prayers should issue from the spirit of ultimate union with all the members of the Body of Christ, although they do not force us to enter that spirit. As a prayer rising from the ultimate depths, and bearing the most true and classical expression of supernatural reality, liturgical prayer possesses an incomparable communion-forming power. For we must not forget that values possess a unifying power; and the higher the value in question, the greater this power. In beholding a value, in grasping it, the soul of the individual is not only "recollected," drawn out of "distraction," but the barrier isolating us from other men is lifted. Every true value, such as the beauty of nature or of a masterpiece of art like Beethoven's Ninth Symphony, or the moral light of a generous act of forgiveness, or of an immovable fidelity, all these values which speak to us of God and touch our hearts, draw our spirit towards the true world of God, lead us before the face of God, and thanks to them, the barriers of pride, egotism and self-assertion, which isolate us and make us look upon our fellow-men from the outside as adversaries and competitors, fall away.

The higher the value, the more we become aware of the ultimate objective unity in God. This fact takes on an entirely new sense when we come to the supernatural world of holiness, and especially when we contemplate Christ, when the glory of Christ, of "the only begotten of the Father, full of grace and truth," touches our heart. We inwardly achieve this objective union as members of the Mystical Body of Christ to the degree that we become inebriated with Christ. For it is not true that the highest "I and thou communion" with Christ destroys communion with other men, causing us to forget others, to have no more place for them in our hearts. On the contrary, inasmuch as we love Jesus, and inasmuch as a mysterious relationship is formed with Him and we lovingly grow into Him, we participate in His love for our neighbor, *amor Christi urget nos*, "the love of Christ impels us," becomes alive in us; we reach that degree of depth where that ultimate personally achieved communion can be formed; in other words, we truly reach the point where we became aware of the ultimate supernatural unity with all men in Christ. It is a specifically liberal Protestant error to believe that the more a thing is peripheral, the more it leads towards the spirit of communion, and that, on the contrary, the deeper we are moved by something and the higher the value in question, the more we are plunged into solitude. The opposite is true. That which satisfies me alone, which bears only upon my own enjoyment, isolates. The world of authentic values, on the contrary, unifies. And God, the deepest theme of each of us, the highest Good, is at the same time the most general theme, of which we cannot be absolutely conscious unless we are also conscious of our ultimate deepest communion with all men.

The atmosphere of the Liturgy is saturated with Christ, with the hidden God revealed in Christ. Not only does it deal with God as do other prayers; more than all else it shows us the ultimate, whole supernatural reality; it speaks from the ultimate truth of the metaphysical situation of man; it reflects God's face in a unique adequateness; it speaks the tongue of Christ; it envelops us in an atmosphere of eternity above all measures of time and space.

Truly, when we stand in this sphere of the Liturgy, when it environs us, we witness the *Phase Domini,* the "Passing of the Lord." In it we touch Christ without any sort of falsification or subjective alteration. It therefore awakens us to that true, ultimate consciousness of communion, that ultimate, conquering union in love, which is the very opposite of all human relationships of easy intimacy. This is the very opposite of an easy familiarity, of the "smug society spirit" which is nothing else but a common falling into the periphery, and only means isolation in the depths. The Liturgy alone, because of its supra-individual stamp, its all-embracing breadth, never violates the separate man's individuality. As for other prayers, it is always possible for them to bear an individual mark and for this reason they cannot be imposed on everybody without an unwarranted pressure. This can be true of the most beautiful prayers of some of the saints, of a Saint Gertrude, for instance, to say nothing of certain hymns whose sentimental and trivial nature is a falsification of the spirit of Christ.

This supra-individual character of the Liturgy is at the same time the very opposite of colorless neu-

trality or of a bloodless stereotype; it combines
holy sobriety with the greatest ardour, eternal calm
with the deepest emotion, holy fear with holy joy,
and winged peace; all these are mingled in that
coincidentia oppositorum, that meeting of opposites
implied only by God, the content of all values, and
in whom all values are contained *per eminentiam,*
because they are "surpassed." Each individuality,
however strongly expressed, can take part in this
supra-individual prayer; and one can take part in
it without having to give up or disavow that special
secret word that God utters anew to each soul, in so
far as the latter represents a unique, induplicable
design of God.

This mysterious principle inherent in the Liturgy
adds to all which it makes it own — the sermon of
each saint, each prayer, even the apostle's epistles
— a deeper beauty and actuality, something that
shines more brightly than these same texts isolated
from their liturgical context. Thus, for instance,
Jeremiah's lamentations in the Tenebrae, or the
words of Saint Paul in the epistle of Holy Saturday: "Brothers, therefore, if you be risen with
Christ, seek the things that are above; where Christ

is sitting at the right hand of God. Mind the things
that are above, not the things that are upon the earth.
For you are dead; and your life is hid with Christ
in God. When Christ shall appear, Who is your
life, then you also shall appear with Him in glory."
With what a new significance, with how much more
mysterious an actuality, do these words shine! Thus
also the words of Saint Leo, Saint Gregory and Saint
Augustine in the Christmas Matins, or Saint Peter's
epistle on Easter Saturday: "But you are a chosen
generation, a kingly priesthood, a holy nation, a
purchased people: that you may declare his virtues
who has called you out of darkness into His marvel-
lous light." (*Vos autem genus electum, regale
sacerdotium, gens sancta, populus acquisitionis:
ut virtutes annuntietis ejus, qui de tenebris vos
vocavit in admirabile lumen suum.*)

The individuality of each saint and apostle differs,
yet the spirit and rhythm of the Liturgy are one.
The spirit of them all is inserted into the Liturgy
in serving it; it brings to light that which is deepest
in their words, pervading it with the rhythm of the
liturgical year. The very words of Our Lord not
only become more comprehensible, but acquire the

background and frame in which they develop in their entire "breadth, length and depth," as words of eternal life.   Think, for instance, of the words accompanying the washing of the feet at Holy Thursday Mass, the words of the Sermon on the Mount at the Mass on All Saints' Day, or those of the Gospel of Pentecost.

The Liturgy also conveys the direct consciousness of the value of communion as such.   I mean the notion that communion is not only valuable in so far as the sanctification of each individual is concerned, which is pointed out often enough, but also because it is precious and valuable in itself, because God is imitated and glorified in it.   The loving communion of the faithful not only engenders the sanctity of individual persons, but it is also the precious fruit of that sanctity, as is mysteriously revealed in the words of Christ to his disciples: "By this shall all men know that you are my disciples, if you have love one for another."   The communion of saints implies a separate new value over and above that of individual saintliness, a value that would be lacking if the world consisted only of saints in no way linked together.

This value of unity as such, and of the victory of love which is manifested in communion, apart from all that it means for individual sanctification, is revealed to us in many passages of the Liturgy, especially in the Epistles of Saint Paul and in the Psalm *Ecce quam bonum et quam iucundum habitare fratres in unum* ("Behold how good and how pleasant it is for brethren to dwell together in unity.")

Apart from this particular value of communion, we behold here *a new dimension of the glorification of God*. "When two or three are assembled in the name of Christ," there appears a new dimension of the lordship of Christ, different from the case in which two persons separate and not linked together adhere to Christ. Of course, the most important thing is the lordship of Christ in each individual soul. But the communion of the Mystical Body of Christ presents its own dimension of the lordship of God and the glorification of God, which is different from the lordship of God in the individual soul — and this quite apart from the fact that the soul of the individual can be ontologically bound to Christ only by becoming a member of His Mystical Body. On the obverse side, a pseudo-community of heretics represents a new evil over and above the mere sum of heretics who are not bound together, for this pseudo-community increases the outrage in the eyes of God.

And the Liturgy is fully and directly awake to this particular value of the Kingdom of God, of the *chorus* of prayer, praise and glorification, beyond the individual prayers of the faithful. This increase of value is not made in terms of numbers and it must not be identified with quantitative categories according to which the individual, being one, appears as far too insignificant. The individual who is the dwelling-place of Christ is also infinitely precious in the eyes of God: "Precious in the eyes of God is the death of His saints." The increase of values rather is in the inter-personal lordship of Christ, in the kingdom of Christ, which is added to the realm of lordship in the individual soul. Fundamentally speaking these are all simply different aspects of the one essential fact of the Mystical Body of Christ. It is obvious that through the Liturgy we constantly grow into this unity and are constantly reminded of it as in no other devotion.

The unique character of communion of the Mysti-

The Liturgical Spirit is an "addition" not a Substitution

cal Body of Christ, is first of all embodied in the liturgical act in the celebration of the holy Sacrifice of the Mass and in the recitation of the Office. I do not speak here of the ontological supernatural formation of all into one, which is accomplished in the unbloody re-presentation of the sacrifice on the cross, of the streams of divine love which objectively put an end to all the divisions and conflicts brought about by sin in man. I mean the ultimate "we," which binds the faithful, the priest and Christ to one another, in the offering of the Holy Mass, the *"we"* which reaches its climax in the common meal at the Lord's table. All receive the one body of the Lord, all are assimilated unto the one Lord. Even if we leave aside the supreme ontological supernatural unity which is realized here, the very act of undergoing this experience represents an incomparable communion-forming power.

And the prayer in common, the self-constituted "we" which is uttered when God is to be praised, thanked or implored, the gesture of the Divine Office as such, is a fulfillment of the communion of the Mystical Body of Christ, an actualization of that deepest, uttermost bond of love and of the common

destiny of guilt, atonement, and sonship in Christ.
One faith, one hope, one love, one longing, one expectation of the day of our Lord!   One vigil, one
joy, one praise!   Everything is built into the realm
of the culminating unity in God.   And this ultimate
character of communion expressed in the Liturgy
appears also in the meaning and atmosphere of its
individual words and thoughts.   Thus for instance,
in the self-evident plural of the *Gaudete*, the *Gaudeamus omnes diem festum celebrantes*, of the
Gloria of Holy Mass: "We praise thee, we bless
thee, we adore thee, we glorify thee", in the *Fratres,
sobrii estote et vigilate*, in the *Pater Noster*, and innumerable other passages.

It is sufficient to recall the prayer *Communicantes*,
before consecration and the *Nobis quoque peccatoribus* after the consecration, or the Secret of the Feast
of Corpus Christi: "Grant to thy Church the gifts
of unity and peace, which are mystically signified
by the gifts which we offer up," the Antiphon during the washing of the feet on Holy Thursday: *Ubi
caritas et amor, Deus ibi est.   Congragavit nos in
unum Christi amor.   Exsultemus, et in ipso iucun-
demur.   Timeamus et amemus Deum vivum.   Et*

ex corde diligamus nos sincero. Simul ergo cum in unum congregamur: Ne nos mente dividamur, caveamus. Cessent iurgia maligna, cessent lites. Et in medio nostri sit Christus Deus. "Where charity and love is, there God is. The love of Christ hath gathered us together in one. Let us rejoice and be glad in him. Let us fear and love the living God. And let us love him with a sincere heart. When therefore we are gathered together in one, let us take heed not to be divided in mind. Let malefic quarrels cease, let all strife cease. And let Christ our God be in the midst of us."

In this spirit of communion embodied in the Liturgy we find one of the most fundamental traits of true personality. An isolated man, one who has not become conscious of the ultimate objective link binding him to all other men before God, is an unawakened, immature, even a mutilated man. That liberal conception which considers the "solitary" man as the great, profound, human being is the logical outcome of the understanding of communion as something peripheral in its nature. Of course, a true personality is solitary among average men because this personality is alone in his knowledge of that deep communion to which average men have not awakened; he is not satisfied with the superficial ties of mere interest or pleasure and seeks a profounder link; he does not inwardly accept the communion offered by the average. But a true personality is never solitary in the sense of being isolated from others in the depths, in the sense of hostility or indifference; he is not unalive to that ultimate, triumphant sense of unity with his brother, whom he sees in the place where each man in truth stands before God, whether he is aware of it or not. The fathers of the desert and the hermits lived entirely in that spirit of true communion, unlike their pagan contemporaries inhabiting crowded cities, surrounded by other men and bound to them by peripheral ties. The true measure of the depth of a man will much rather be found in whether or not he is awakened to that spirit of true communion, in whether or not there has been a breaking down of the inner walls of self-assertion, the defences of the sphere of his own ego.

The shutting up of oneself in this inner fortress of egotism, which exists secretly even in the most jovial joiner of clubs, is proof of narrowness, limitation,

even stupidity. For it presupposes a certain egocentric attitude towards the world and God. The
man who has been melted by the sun of values, and
above all the man who has been wounded by the
love of Christ, is also lovingly open to every man
and has entered into the objective unity of all. Yes,
this ultimate true spirit of communion, the universal
disposition to love and the life in the ultimate loving we, is only possible as a fruit of the ultimate "I-
and-thou communion" with Christ, through which
we are transfigured into Christ. Every attempt to
achieve this *"we"* without Christ leads to a superficially anchored pseudo-communion. It suffices to
recall, for instance, the humanitarian ideal. Every
attempt to achieve a *"we"* which does not pass
through the "thou" of the God-Man, fails to achieve
the full conquest of egocentricity; on the contrary,
it leads to a mass-egotism, which is perhaps even
lower than the egotism of the individual in its pre-
tension to be an ultimate liberation from the im-
prisonment of self.

Thus we see, that the Liturgy draws us quite obviously and organically into that true spirit of communion which is the indispensable foundation of

true personality.   It leads us through Christ to the "I-and-thou" communion with our brother and to the ultimate "we-communion" of humanity in the Mystical Body of Christ.   In itself it leads us through Christ into the presence of God, where there is no more *isolation* and no more separation.   The Liturgy not only teaches us about this communion, and it is not only offered to us as a commandment, but it is plainly achieved in the common adoring sacrifice, praise and prayer, in the common reception of God's grace, and all *per Christum Dominum Nostrum.*

V

THE SPIRIT OF REVERENCE IN THE LITURGY

A man is rich in values, is a personality in the highest sense of the word, to the degree that he perceives values and possesses a spiritual vision clear and open to the fullness of the world of values, above all to the world of supernatural values; to the degree that the gift of himself to the realm of values is pure and absolute, and above all the self-surrender to Christ and through Christ to God. Reverence is the essential basis for such a perception of values and for a true relationship with the whole realm of values, with what is above and what speaks from "above," with the Absolute, the supernatural and the divine. Reverence is the mother of all virtues, of all religion. It is the foundation and the beginning because it enables our spirit to possess real knowledge, and primarily the knowledge of values. It is that fundamental attitude towards being in which one gives all being the opportunity to unfold

itself in its specific nature, in which one neither behaves as its master nor acts arrogantly towards it.

In its most primitive form reverence is a response
to the general value of being as such, to the dignity
which all being possesses as opposed to nothing or
to mere fictitiousness, to the value of its own consistency, of standing on its own, of the ultimate
"positivity" of being.   In this right and appropriate
attitude towards being as such, this affirmation free
from obtrusiveness, this silent, contemplative disposition towards being as being, the world begins
to disclose itself in its entire depth, differentiation
and plenitude of value.   Every newly disclosed
value creates a new form, enrichment and differentiation of reverence.   So, too, every newly evolved
form of reverence, and consequently, every new response of reverence to the newly disclosed values,
open and widen our outlook, enabling us to grasp
new values and to understand better those which
are already known.   Reverence is thus the foundation of all perception and sense of values.   But it
is also an indispensable element of every response to
value, or in other words, it is a fundamental component of a true relationship with the world of values.

It represents the proper answer to the majesty of values, to the "message" they convey to us of God, that of the absolute, the infinitely superior. Only the person who possesses reverence is capable of real enthusiasm, of joy in so far as it is motivated by values, true love and obedience. The man who lacks reverence is blind to values and incapable of submission to them.

The lack of reverence may have two roots, and accordingly there are two different types of men wanting in reverence: the arrogant person and the senseless, blunt one. The first root is to be found in pride. The man who lacks reverence because of pride and arrogance approaches everything with conceit and presumption, imagines that he knows everything, that he sees through everything. He is interested in the world only in so far as it serves his self-glorification, in so far as it enhances his own importance. He does not take being seriously in itself and he leaves things no spiritual room to unfold their own essences. He thinks himself always greater than that which is not himself. The world holds no mystery for him. He treats everything tactlessly, with easy familiarity, and everything seems to him to be at his disposal. To his insolent, conceited gaze, to his despotic approach, the world is sealed, silent, bared of all mystery, deprived of all depth, flat, and limited to one dimension. He stands in desolate emptiness, blind to all the values and secrets of being, circling endlessly around himself.

There is however another form of irreverence born from concupiscence. The concupiscent man is interested in the world only as a means in procuring him pleasure. His is a dominating position in the face of being, not because he wills domination as such, but in order to use being for his pleasure. He, too, circles around in the narrowness of his own self. He does not face the world with arrogance and conceit, but with a blunt stupidity. Stubbornly imprisoned in his own self, he violates being, and seeing it only from the outside, he thus misses its true meaning. Neither to this type of the irreverent does the world disclose its breadth, height, and depth, its richness of values and mysteries.

The reverent man, disposed to know something higher than himself and his pleasure, and willing to submit to it and to abandon himself, the man who grasps his metaphysical situation and lives it, is not only capable of perceiving values and open to the mysteries of being. Such a man is open first of all to the Absolute, or, in other words, he does not shut himself off from the Fact of all Facts, from the existence of God, the absolute Lord. Without this reverence, there is no religion, not even primitive, natural religion. Reverence is not an attitude like humility which appears only as a fruit of the true image of God, as reflected in the face of Christ and presented to us by the Church. It is, at least in its primitive form, the pre-supposition of faith, a *praeambulum fidei*. In antiquity, we find a deep reverence not only in Socrates and Plato, but also in the ethos of the people. How deep was the consciousness of the unrighteousness which lies in Hybris, in this failure of reverence, in this unbridled self-assertion, in this loud and false security! For humility, on the contrary, there is no place in the ancient world. The fear of God which the Scriptures say is the beginning of wisdom (*initium sapientiae timor Domini*) in itself presupposes this fundamental reverence.

Reverence in its primitive form is not only the

basis of every religion, and, above all, of the receptiveness to the *Lumen Christi*, the reception of the word of God, but it is also a constitutive element of hope, faith and love of God. Complete, fully ripened reverence is a component of a true relationship with God, and specifically with the God of revelation. How often, even in a religious man, do we find mixed in with his relations to God a certain self-satisfaction, as in the case of all sentimentality directed towards God, or else a certain familiarity with God, a false, clumsy self-complacency. There are also cases in which such categories as mere formal loyalty, correctness, propriety are insinuated into relations with God, the Eternal, All-Holy and Inscrutable.

All this means a lack of reverence. The significance of reverence for the full personality can easily be conceived. The greatest natural "endowment," the greatest latitude of talents and capacities, can never lead to true personality if reverence is lacking. For the latter is the basis of the second essential component of personality, the perceiving of values, an organic contact with the world of values,

and first of all, the dying to oneself, the preparation
of inner room for Christ.

The man without reverence is necessarily flat and
limited. This lack is an essential mark of stupidity.
Even he whose mind is obdurate and helpless but
possesses reverence, does not manifest that importunate, insolent stupidity of which it is said that "even
the Gods struggle against it in vain." The lack of
reverence is a specific defect of our modern age.
On the one hand, the feeling of reverence is under-
mined by the increasing technicalization and instrumentalization of the world wherein everything is
considered only as a means for the attainment of
practical aims, and being is not allowed to be taken
seriously. On the other hand, the attitude of self-
glorification is increased in man by progress in the
knowledge of secondary causes and by the conquest
of the physical world. This makes us forget that
"He has made us and we have not made ourselves."
It makes the shortsighted intoxicated with superficial
knowledge so that they overlook the *Causa prima*
because of the *causae secundae*. This specifically
involves the stupidity of irreverence, the "short cir-

cuit" of the spirit to which the irreverent man falls
victim.   According to this ultimate criterion, the
most primitive people who ignore all *causae se-*
cundae and link everything directly to God the *Causa*
prima are infinitely closer to truth than the modern
man who has ceased to perceive the deepest meaning
and basis of all things, as he is completely absorbed
by all that is secondary.   In this ultimate sense, the
irreverent modern man, in spite of all his knowledge, is far more "stupid" than the most primitive
savage possessing reverence.   To this fading away
of reverence is linked the peculiar triteness and
levelling of our entire modern life.

Yet it is not the ethos of reverence as such which is
the decisive point, but reverence as an adequate response to the true God.

This is not a misty reverence of a vague consciousness as found in primitive people; it is not the
reverence inspired by the rustle of holy trees or by
an immersion into the biological, seemingly more
powerful than ourselves.   Above all, it is not the
pseudo-reverence expressed in different pantheisms,
the shrinking consciousness of an immensity in
which we are but a drop.   Nor is it the noble rever-

ence of a Socrates before the daimon, or a Plato, which is only an expectation, an obscure questioning fading away in the All.   It is the illuminated, conscious reverence which clearly grasps its object and is formed by the latter's infinite and manifest greatness, its mysterious, inconceivable depths, by the infinite fullness of its values.

The Liturgy is penetrated more than any other devotion by the spirit of true reverence, and it draws those who live it directly into this spirit.   It represents the right, fundamental relation with God and the created, and leads to the classical attitude towards God through Christ.   It is deeply permeated by the fear of God, by the *cum timore et tremore*, and at the same time by the consciousness that we are sons of God, in which we call *"Abba,* Father!"   It is full of the spirit of *servire Domino in laetitia,* to serve God in joy.   In the beginning of Matins, the Church chants the *Invitatorium* psalm which not only puts before our mind our own nothingness before God's majesty, our absolute dependence on Him, the fact that we belong to Him, but in praying it, we live this truth.   *Quoniam Deus magnus Dominus, et Rex magnus super omnes deos: quoniam non repellet*

Dominus plebem suam, quia in manu eius sunt omnes fines terrae, et altitudines montium ipse conspicit.

Quoniam ipsius est mare, et ipse fecit illud, et aridam fundaverunt manus eius: venite adoremus et procidamus ante Deum: ploremus coram Domino, qui fecit nos, quia ipse est Dominus Deus noster: nos autem populus eius, et oves pascuae eius.

(For the Lord is a great God, and a great King above all gods. For in his hands are all the ends of the earth: and the heights of the mountains are his.

For the sea is his, and he made it: and his hands formed the dry land. Come, let us adore and fall down: and weep before the Lord that made us. For he is the Lord our God: and we are the people of his pasture and the sheep of his hand.)

The entire Liturgy is pervaded with this reverence before the *Majestas Domini*, the clear consciousness of His absolute dominion, and the acknowledgement that we receive all from Him. And yet this is no Jansenist or Calvinist remoteness from God. It is not a feeling of being crushed by God's greatness, an annihilating disdain for ourselves, but the *Introibo ad altare Dei, ad Deum, qui laetificat juventutem meam* (I will go in unto the altar of God, unto God, who giveth joy to my youth). It is the *quoniam in aeternum misericordia eius* (for His mercy is in eternity), the *Gustate et videte quam suavis est Dominus* (taste and see how sweet is the Lord), the *Misericordia Domini cantabo in aeternum* (I shall sing through in eternity the Lord's mercy). Let us recall the upward glance which marks the beginning of each day, the *Deus in adjutorium meum intende, Domine ad adjuvandum me festina,* how especially when these words are sung we are permeated with the deepest reverence before God and aware of the true situation of the creature in relation to God. We are drawn into the rhythm of reverence of the praying Church. How strong the spirit of reverence in the Preface and the *Sanctus,* a reverence which is at the same time linked to the consciousness that we are sons of God. The spirit of reverence is also expressed in the fact that in all our orisons we never turn directly to God but always address Him through the One, in Whom alone God is well pleased, *per*

Christum Dominum nostrum. This feeling that we only dare address God in Christ and through Christ is one deeply opposed to all easy familiarity and to dealing with God without observing distances.

The Holy Sacrifice of the Mass is especially penetrated with this spirit, the necessity of sacrificing to God, the impossibility of offering Him an adequate sacrifice because of our poverty, the sacrificial prayer of Christ in which we are allowed to participate, the primal, classical attitude before God, the *per ipsum, cum ipso et in ipso est tibi, Deo patri omnipotenti in unitate Spiritus Sancti, omnis honor et gloria,* (By him, and with him, and in him, is to thee God the Father almighty, in the unity of the Holy Ghost all honour and glory).

We find this spirit, too, toward all that enters in contact with the Lord's Holy Body, in the handling of the paten and the cleansing of the chalice. We also find it in all that symbolizes Christ or is dedicated to the divine service, in the kissing of the divine altar and the Gospel. It is expressed in the bodily comportment of the priest, the faithful and the religious; in the standing up during the reading of the Gospels, the songs of praise from the Gospel, the

Magnificat, Benedictus, Nunc Dimittis, in the bowing of the head during the *Gloria Patri.* The very fact of the harmonious structure and order of the entire Liturgy, reflected even in its outer comportment, contains a profound element of reverence. This peculiar organic structure, corresponding so clearly to the inner attitude of standing before God, is the very opposite of slackness, and at the same time it has nothing to do with the attitude of a military or athletic drill.

He who lives in the Liturgy becomes filled with reverence not only in the sense of that fundamental reverence which is a *praeambulum fidei,* a precondition of faith, but also in the sense of that reverence which is a part of faith in the Triune God, hope in God, love of God — in other words, the reverence of the God-man Jesus Christ Himself.

The formation of personality by the Liturgy, as explained here means not only the moulding of what is most central in the human person, his right relation towards God. It also means the moulding of correct relations towards all realms of being and every kind of value. It means the formation of the whole man. Even when we are concerned with

realms of being not expressly mentioned in the Liturgy, our correct attitude towards God must serve
us as a *causa exemplaris,* a model for our attitude
towards all values.

The man formed by the Liturgy is reverent towards
his fellow-man, in whom he sees, if he is a member
of the Mystical Body of Christ, a "second Christ,"
or if he is not yet "reborn" a soul destined to be thus
reborn, and transformed into Christ.   The words
of Christ, "As long as you did it to one of these my
least brethren, you did it to me," disclose to us the
holy, reverence-inspiring plenitude which lives in
every Christian.   Above all, the human being acquires an extraordinary worth through the Incarnation of the Eternal Word, the Second Divine Person.   It may be said that our faith in Christ leads
us directly to this reverence for man.   He who lives
the true Catholic faith, and not he alone who lives
in the Liturgy, possesses this reverence for his fellow-
man.   Surely, the Liturgy does not teach us anything new beyond that which is already included in
the *Credo.   But the Liturgy is accomplished faith,
lived faith.*   It plunges us into the full reality of the
truth of faith; it creates the spiritual space in which

the world of faith or, more correctly, the world disclosed by faith, penetrates every pore of our being, in
which we breathe the supernatural air and touch ontologically this reality in the Holy Sacrifice of the
Mass and in the sacraments. It builds up that sacred
sense of communion, already described by us, which
is entirely steeped in reverence. The unifying
power here is Christ Himself, and our link with
other men necessarily implies our consideration of
our brother as a vessel of grace.

There are certain non-liturgical forms of community among the faithful, where in spite of a common faith the plane on which we unite is quite distinct from the supernatural. In numerous Catholic
associations, despite their high practical significance, fellowship is too often born out of social or
professional interests; their atmosphere is made up
of cosiness and smugness, joviality, jollity, in which
the other is considered as playing a social rôle, as
a comrade, a *Kommilitone,* or at best as one shar-
ing the same "view of life." The abundance and
depth of the spiritual person, in so far as he is a
creature made in the image of Christ, and especially
"membership" in the Mystical Body of Christ and

the fact of being sons of God, are effaced in their consciousness and do not play the part of a real, achieved element in the sense of communion. In such unions the spirit of reverence towards our brothers cannot be formed in us, the kind of spirit which we directly acquire in the Liturgy and which rings out to us in the Epistle of Easter Saturday: "But you are a chosen generation, a kingly priesthood, a holy nation, a purchased people."

The man formed by the Liturgy is also reverent towards his own body. He regards it as "the temple of the Holy Ghost." This simple truth of supernatural life is achieved in the Liturgy. Let us recall the rites of baptism, holy anointing and confirmation.

The attitude of reverence is especially opposed to all pragmatic conduct. The contrary of a reverential attitude towards being results when everything is considered only as a means, as an instrument for subjective and fortuitous aims; all is used as a coin against which something can be exchanged; nothing is taken seriously for its own sake; nothing is ever conceived in its function of imitating God, in

its inner nobleness, in its objective, God-willed vocation, its destination to serve the higher.

The Liturgy naturally leads us to an attitude of
reverence towards all that is created, even towards
pure matter, in the great classical display of all
things *in conspectu Dei.* The Liturgy considers all
things, water, fire, wax, bread, wine, oil, salt, the
sea, the mountains, as images of the endless fullness
of God in their inner preciousness and also in their
mysterious symbolism in the supernatural order.

A unique perspective of the cosmos appears each
time the Liturgy speaks expressly of a created thing:
the industrious bee in the *Exsultat* of Holy Saturday; water and fire in the rites of their blessing; a
new dimension of depth is disclosed in these created
things, a dimension quite different from the blunt
one we are accustomed to in our daily lives. They
are aglow with the light of that mystery of the heights
which inhabits every being in so far as it has been
born from the touch of God's finger. This aspect
is the fertile ground for a deep reverence towards
all that is — in accordance with the hierarchy of
being — and the cosmos as a whole.

VI

THE SPIRIT OF RESPONSE-TO-VALUE IN THE LITURGY

We have already seen that the second component in the formation of personality consists in the perceiving of value and the person's fundamental response-to-value. To express it in other words, the intentional foundation of the formation of personality and of the transformation into Christ is the apprehension of and the response to value. To be irradiated and touched by values, to affirm and give oneself up to all that which possesses a value and to be joyous and enthusiastic over them, above all to love them, is to be wed to the world of values whereby we become transformed and the fullness of personal values blossoms out in us. In the adoring love of the God who discloses himself in Christ we become like Christ; the life of Christ ontologically implanted in us by baptism develops personally in us.

The very soul of the response-to-value is the consciousness that an adequate response is due to each value suitable to its rank. The motive of the response-to-value should never be the desire to bring about the transformation of the person, but to give to the value its due response.

This was seen before when the aim with which the Liturgy is performed was examined. One of the most elementary truths is involved here. It may be expressed as follows: to every value an adequate response is due on the part of the person *because it is a value.* This response should not be given in order that something might come out of it or be realized through it. Nor should it be given in the name of this or that purpose. Indeed, there is an ultimate, cosmic value in the suitable response to every value, and a ultimate cosmic non-value, a disharmony, in the lack of response or in a false response. This cosmic value has nothing to do with the personal value involved in the right response. The personal value is something new beyond the value represented by the fact that the right response is given, and indeed presupposes this cosmic value. The cosmic non-value exists even when a value — a moral person, for instance — does not receive the adequate response of love and respect because it is

misunderstood through no fault of the one who mis-
understands.   The cosmic value of the objective fact
that every value should receive an adequate response
of will, joy, enthusiasm, love, according to the kind
of value it represents finds its highest, ultimate *causa
exemplaris* in the eternal loving response between
the first and second Divine Persons.

This primary fact that to every value an adequate
response is due on the part of the person, because
the value is such as it is cannot be demonstrated or
deduced from something else; it is something ultimate which we can only apprehend directly.   This
primary fact finds its highest expression in the
response-to-value of adoring love and glorification
of God Who includes all values.

One of the most essential elements of true personality is the consciousness that we owe to values
a due response.   By this the *theocentric* man is distinguished from the *egocentric* one.   Shut up in
himself, the egocentric man is incapable of this self-
abandon.   He is incapable of giving himself up to
the world saturated with value and meaning simply
for its own sake and for no other reason.   He is
incapable of soaring with the objective logos.   The

purely egocentric man, dominated entirely by pride
or concupiscence, is generally blind to values, has
no contact with them and their inner life, and is also
without contact with God Who includes all values.
The proud man is hostile to values. The concupiscent man is indifferent to them. The proud man
hates God and denies him expressly in an impotent
revolt. The concupiscent man ignores God.

But there exist less extreme forms of egocentrism.
Among them is the type of man who is capable of
perceiving values and penetrating them, but always
looks back on himself. He will never obey the demand of giving a suitable response to value simply
because such a response is due to it and for no other
reason. He will help another man only in order to
grow morally himself and not in the name of love.
He approaches beauty in order to attain spiritual
culture. He prays to God in order to achieve religious progress. Of course, our own person also
demands that we should manifest toward it a responding-to-value interest, that we should affirm the
immanent design of God in us and seek its full
development. We must first of all affirm the
supernatural life bestowed on us through baptism

and seek its full unfolding. But this precisely means to be responsive to values and not to look back on the value attached to this response while it is being given; it means to live wholly in the objective value confronting us. It means that while giving the response we fix our gaze only on the value in question, without casting a side-glance, without "squinting," so that we may perceive at the same time the act of response being accomplished. Here it is of no importance whether we ourselves, another man, an event, or a thing are the objects of this response. When we reject our own negative-values in contrition and at the same time "revoke" our past unworthy conduct, our comportment is as objectively directed as that of loving another human being. Contrariwise, the egocentric man, in manifesting contrition, casts a side-glance and "squints" at his own contrition; he will even "relish" his moral attitude instead of being absorbed in the sorrow he experiences because of his past conduct. While examining his conscience, he will take satisfaction in his piety.

When this egocentric type encounters a value, as in beholding something beautiful or meeting a noble

man, he will see in all this but an opportunity for
ascetic exercises, instead of taking interest in the
value as such, responding to it as a reflection of God,
and forgetting himself and giving himself up to God
Who speaks to us after His own fashion in all true
values. This egocentric type will help his neighbour, not because this help is due to him, nor because he must testify to the truth that the hungry
and thirsting Christ stands before him, but because
he seeks to accomplish a meritorious act. The egocentric type does not pray to God because the glory
of God brings him down to his knees, because God
is infinitely glorious, inconceivably holy and great,
nor because he understands that this response is due
to the King of eternal glory. He prays to God because he wants to become more perfect, acquire
merits and gain graces. In short, somehow the egocentric man transforms his giving himself up to value
into a means for his own perfection whereby he is
not interested in this perfection because of the glorification of God but because it is *his own* perfection.

The more free from egocentrism a man is, the
more is he a personality. Every form of egocentrism, of being shut up in oneself, is narrowness,

pettiness, limitation, a cutting off of oneself from the sources of all true life, indeed from God Himself.   The egocentric tendency empties all response-to-value of its content, de-substantializes it, disturbs the wedding with values, and hence the inner transformation of the person, the richness in values which the person acquires through response-to-value and from it.

The egocentric type is in a tragic situation.   For he will never achieve his own fullness of values which he seeks, demands and wants to enjoy.   The more he demands, the less will he obtain.   For only when the response-to-value is given to its object purely because it is a value can this fullness in value be achieved, only when the person is penetrated with the consciousness that this response is objectively due to the value.   Such a fullness in values can be achieved only through self-forgetfullness, by not instrumentalizing the response-to-value, by not "squinting" at the fullness achieved by the self, "letting not thy left hand know what thy right hand doeth," according to the Gospel.

To such men may be applied the words of Christ, "Amen I say to you, they have received their reward." In the utterance, "He that shall lose his life shall find it," shines the exalted truth that the person is rich in values to the extent that he gives himself up in pure response to the world of values, and first of all to God Who contains all values. A man is more of a personality, in the highest sense of the word, the less he seeks to turn life into an "art," the less he troubles about his own cultivation. He is the more a personality, the more he progresses in giving himself up to values, and especially in self-forgetfullness and complete sacrifice to God. The creative primary gesture of personality-formation is the pure gift of oneself to the value as such, without the commingling of anything egocentric.

In the Liturgy we find embodied in unique fashion the spirit of true response-to-value, this awareness (the antithesis of egocentrism), that an adequate answer is due to value because it is such as it is. Not in the name of this or that aim, nor in order to achieve improvement or sanctification of ourselves, but *quoniam to solus Sanctus, tu solus Dominus, tu solus Altissimus* (For thou only art holy. Thou only art Lord. Thou only art most high.) Before the Gospel, the *Gloria tibi, Domine!* (Glory be to thee, O Lord!) is repeated.   Before the Preface, the *Gratias agamus Domino, Deo Nostro* (Let us give thanks unto the Lord our God) is recited, and the answer is: *Vere dignum et justum est* (It is truly meet and just).   Before the *Pater Noster: Per ipsum et cum ipso et in ipso est tibi, Deo Patri omnipotenti, in unitate Spiritus Sancti, omnis honor et gloria* (By him, and with him, and in him, is to thee, God the Father almighty, in the unity of the Holy Ghost all honour and glory).

The Holy Sacrifice of the Mass as a whole is the primary fulfillment of adoration and love which gives itself and sacrifices itself completely.   The sacrificial love of the God-Man, the gift of Himself to the Heavenly Father, is the primal theocentric attitude.   And inasmuch as a man is inwardly formed through participation in the Holy Sacrifice of the Mass, all egocentric deviation from response-to-value is bound to disappear.   The spirit which breathes in the Holy Mass is penetrated with the primary fact that the response of adoring and atoning love is due to God's endless majesty and holiness. Likewise the various thoughts and words are filled with this truth.   The *Gloria* clearly expresses it:

Gratias agimus tibi propter magnam gloriam tuam (We give thee thanks for thy great glory).

The sequence of the Hours as a whole also testifies to the primary fact that we owe God this expressed glorification, *propter magnam gloriam suam.* The individual parts likewise are penetrated with this idea that "we must" praise, glorify and thank God; they convey the inner significance of this response which in no way bears the character of a means. First of all, the *Gloria Patri, et Filio, et Spiritui Sancto,* (Glory be to the Father, and to the Son and to the Holy Ghost) which marks all the hours of the day, the *Domine, labia mea aperies: et os meum annuntiabit laudem tuam* (O Lord, thou will open my lips: and my mouth shall declare they praise), the *Venite, adoremus, et procidamus ante Deum* (Come, let us adore and fall down before the Lord), in the *Invitatorium* Psalm, the *Te Deum* at the end of Matins, the Song of Praise of the three youths in the fiery furnace, the *Laudate* psalm in the Lauds, the *Benedictus* in the Lauds, the *Magnificat* in the Vespers, and innumerable other passages of the psalms and antiphons. Suffice it to recall the *Laudate Dominus omnes gentes* (O praise the Lord, all

ye nations), the *Laudate pueri Dominum* (Praise
the Lord, ye children), the *Ecce nunc benedicite Dominum* of the Compline, the *Quam admirabile est
nomen tuum Domine super terram* (How admirable
is thy name in the whole earth), the *Quam magni-
ficata sunt opera tua Domine* (How magnified art
Thy works O Lord!), and many, many others. The
Doxology concluding every hymn conveys in the
most express manner the consciousness that this
response is due to God. The same can be said of
the *Te decet laus, te decet hymnus!* at the end of
the monastic Matins.

The person formed by the Liturgy has absorbed
in his flesh and blood the notion that he owes a suitable response to every value. He will rejoice in
every exalted spectacle of nature, the beauty of the
starlit sky, the majesty of the sea and mountains,
the charm of life, the world of plants and animals,
the nobility of a profound truth, the mysterious glow
of a man's purity, the victorious goodness of a
fervent neighbourly love. The man formed by the
Liturgy will affirm all this as a reflection of the
eternal glory of God, and not with the thought that
it is meant for his own satisfaction or that through

such an affirmation he will develop and grow inwardly. It will be on his part a spontaneous accomplishment of what is due, the realization of the fact that he owes this response to all that has a value, that the value in question objectively "deserves" this response. Nor will it be on his part the fulfillment of a painful duty, but a spontaneous gift of himself to the value, a blissful acquiescence in the lovable beauty of the value, a gladdening submission to the Lord of whom it is said *Gustate et videte quod suavis est Dominus,* (O taste and see that the Lord is sweet). The person formed by the Liturgy will not ask himself whether he is obliged under sin to give this response. His entire value-responding attitude, his heart and spirit will be turned completely towards the world of values and God in the first place. By this he will speak: *Vultum tuum quaesivi Domine* (I have sought thy face, O Lord). He will achieve this response freely from within, and even experience it as the highest of all bliss.

Here it should be understood that the awareness of the fact that an adequate response is due to each value, that it does not depend on our choice whether we give a response and what response we give, as for example it depends on our choice whether we prefer a warm or cool room, is closely linked to the attraction of the glow of values, the "enchantment" inspired by the inner beauty of values.   This awareness of the world of values and finally of God, this fact that we owe a response of love and joy, has nothing to do with any neutral feeling of duty that goes against the heart's inclination; it is organically bound with the longing for union with each thing that possesses value which speaks to us of the glory of God, and especially with the longing for union with God Himself.   Such a longing is an essential element of every response-to-value, and primarily of love.

The full conforming to values, as it is expressed above all in the central response-to-value of love, implies not only the affirmation of the value in itself, the *Gratias agimus tibi propter magnam gloriam tuam,* but also the longing for union with the object of value, the spiritual "hastening" towards the beloved, in which the unique giving up of one's own person is achieved.   And just this *full* response-to-value is *due* to God.   The *Vultum tuum quaesivi* must build itself up organically on the *Gratias agi-mus tibi propter magnam gloriam tuam*. Other-wise the response-to-value would not be complete. To see a selfish motive behind this longing for union would be to fall victim to a grave error. It would imply the failure to see clearly how this longing bases itself necessarily on the affirmation itself and how the giving up of oneself is completely achieved in it. Of course, here also an inner sequence must be observed. In the first place there must be the pure response-to-value affirmation which appears in its highest form in loving adoration, from which "the serving of God" flows forth. Then only does the turning towards union follow. The essence of the *intentio unionis* is not the *longing,* that is the striving towards something which has not yet been fulfilled, but the concern with union which is also continued in Eternity where "all is fulfilled." It is a specific lack of classicism, a lack of understanding of the ultimate, organic relationships, to see an egocentric element in this striving towards union which es-sentially belongs to love. The Liturgy teaches us that this striving belongs to the true relationship with God, that God demands from us not only adoration

but also love, and that He himself loves us with this
love.   The longing to touch God, the will to attain
Him, is a profoundly legitimate element of the liturgical act, and is even necessary for the full glorification of God.   This loving motion is essentially
embedded in the gesture of glorification which the
God-Man performs in regard to His Heavenly Father.

The eternal union with God is also a theme of the
Liturgy.   It suffices to recall the already mentioned
Quaesivi vultum tuum of the Introit of the Sunday
in the octave of the Ascension, or the *Unam petii a
Domino hanc requiram, ut inhabitem in domo Domini omnibus diebus vitae meae* (One thing I have
asked of the Lord, this will I seek after; that I may
dwell in the house of the Lord all the days of my
life), or the *Sitivit in te anima mea* (My soul panteth
after Thee), and the "As the hart panteth after the
fountains of water, so my soul panteth after thee, O
God.   My soul hath thirsted after the strong living
God.   When shall I come and appear before the
face of God?"   All of Advent is penetrated with
this loving longing which is so movingly expressed
by Saint John in the concluding lines of the Apoca-

lypse: *Veni Domine Jesu* (Come, Lord Jesus). This loving longing grows ever more intense until it reaches the *Rorate coeli desuper* (Drop down dew, ye heavens) and the *Veni Domine et noli tardare* (Come, O Lord, and do not delay) of the Fourth Sunday of Advent.

But this element manifests itself especially in Holy Communion in which the God-Man comes to us in ineffable manner and unites Himself to us in a way which is far beyond all the possibilities of natural union: *Qui manducat meam carnem et bibit meum sanguinem, manet in me et ego in eo* (He that eateth my flesh, and drinketh my blood abideth in me, and I in him); *Desiderio desideravi comedere hoc pascha vobiscum* (With desire I have desired to eat this pasch with you). And He says this to us in every Communion. But in the Communion of the Quinquagesima Sunday the Church sings: *Non sunt fraudati a desiderio suo* (They were not defrauded of that which they craved).

It would also be a misunderstanding of the true nature of theocentrism to seek to exclude one's own person as entirely unessential. As we have already seen on different occasions, man must imitate and

glorify God through his own being, through the fullness of values which blossom out in him. That
Christ should be imitated in a man, and that the
unique, unduplicable design of God represented by
this man should achieve its complete development,
is a great thing in God's eyes. We become strik-
ingly aware of this when we consider what the Credo
says: *Qui propter nos homines et propter nostram
salutem descendit de coelis* (Who for us men,
and for our salvation, came down from heaven).
What is so extraordinarily significant in the eyes of
God should be as significant in our own eyes. It
would not be fully and genuinely to "tread before
God," sacrifice to Him, adoringly praise Him, glorify Him and pray to Him, if this confrontation between man and God did not take place, a confrontation wherein is put the question: "Who art thou and
who am I?"

There are, moreover, defenders of a false theocentrism who believe that one should entirely forget
how one is and what one is, in order to rejoice only
in the glory of God. This leads to an unserious,
one might say, an aestheticized attitude towards God,
looking as a spectator upon Him, forgetting that one

stands before the Lord of Life and Death, before *Our Lord,* to Whom we belong, to Whom we owe an account. This dropping of one of the partners in the relationships with God is absolutely unclassical. The Liturgy knows nothing of it. Of course our first response to objects of value must be their affirmation, a joy in their existence as such. But then the true response-to-value raises the question, "And what about me, can I bear what this value conveys to me of God?" This involves the consciousness of one's own unworthiness and guilt. There are men for whom this last question predominates over all others, so much so that instead of rejoicing in the *magnalia Dei,* the great deeds of God which are revealed in a saint, they feel despondent, saying to themselves: "How different I am! Shall I ever be like him?" This is of course a false and unhealthy attitude. Likewise incorrect is that other attitude wherein we only see the value in itself, without understanding the word which God speaks to us through it, without hearing God's call to us which is also contained in it. The right attitude in contemplating a saint is to rejoice first, in the *magnalia Dei,* to experience this joy and gratitude without troubling about what we are ourselves; and then to take into account the word of God which is spoken to us through him, and to say with St. Augustine: *Si isti cur non ego?* (If these, then why not I?).

The Liturgy breathes this spirit.   In the beginning of the Mass, the priest recites the *Introibo ad altare Dei, ad Deum qui laetificat juventutem meam.* Then follows the confrontation with God, the necessary consequence of the true standing before God, the *Confiteor*, the acknowledgement of one's sins. Only after the appeal to God's mercy, the prayer *Misereatur* (May almighty God have mercy), the asking for forgiveness, and the *Kyrie*, does the *Gloria* follow, wherein once more the pure glorification of God is given expression.   Before the Gospel, we again hear the prayer of purification uttered by the priest or deacon: *Munda cor meum ac labia mea, omnipotens Deus, qui labia Isaiae prophetae calculo mundasti ignito* (Cleanse my heart and my lips, O God almighty, who didst cleanse the lips of the prophet Isaias with a live coal).   Only then does he dare to undertake the reading of the Gospel.

Soon after Transubstantiation, this confrontation of our soul and God takes place once more in the

prayer, *Nobis quoque peccatoribus.* The first part
of the *Pater Noster*, is but a movement towards God's
glory and a full affirmation of this glory in itself, an
act of adoration and glorification, *Sanctificetur nomen tuum; adveniat regnum tuum, fiat voluntas tua*
(Hallowed be thy name; thy kingdom come; thy
will be done). This is followed by the second part,
in which we pray for the forgiveness of our sins, for
absolution and purification. Then comes the *Agnus
Dei, miserere nobis, dona nobis pacem*, the *Domine
non sum dignus*, and then again in the prayer before
the blessing, expressing above all the glory of God,
the final words about eternal welfare.

These are not contradictory elements, nor are they
two paths lying side by side. They are components
of the mutual relationship between man and God
in its organic structure, its classical order of attitudes which cannot be separated and belong to a full,
true glorification, all formed from within by the
rhythm of glorification.

In the person formed by the Liturgy, in the true
personality, the pure response-to-value affirmation
of all true values will predominate. He will rejoice and be filled with enthusiasm at the conversion

of some one, the nobility of a holy friendship, the exalted character of truth, the beauty of nature, the greatness and depth of a work of art; he will affirm God's glory reflected in these things and thank the Lord "because of His great glory." And he will understand that he owes the value the adequate response which is objectively due to it. But out of this affirmation and understanding there will grow in an organic way the longing to come into touch with the *value*, the desire to enter into the truth, to establish a communion with the noble person, to be immersed in the beautiful. Of course, for special reasons, he may renounce this contact in the name of God, in order to make place for God Who contains all values. But in itself the longing for communion with the value and with the world of God revealed in it is linked to the primary rhythm of response-to-value, the pure affirmation of value in itself. If this were lacking, then the value-responding affirmation would not be complete and full-blooded, it would be a mere acknowledgement instead of a giving up of oneself.

The complete and genuine man will also understand the word which God speaks to him in every value, the call of the *sursum corda* addressed to him; he will achieve that confrontation of himself with values which led St. Peter to exclaim before the revelation of the divine power of Christ: "Depart from me, for I am a sinful man, O Lord!"

So many fail, especially in our days, to hear that "call" which God addresses to us in every value. Never in the history of humanity have there been so many "spectators" of God and of the world of values. I refer to the people who are enthusiastic about the Church but do not grasp the *tua res agitur,* "this thing concerns *you,*" which is implied for each of us in the existence of the Church. There are people for example who are full of admiration for a St. Francis of Assisi but do not realize that their own attitudes and modes of life are so profoundly opposed to that world of this saint that they should look upon it as an intolerable reproach to themselves. Such, too, are those for whom Christ is no longer a scandal, not because they belong to Him and obey His call, but because they live so much as spectators that they no longer undertake any "confrontation" with that which stands before them, because they are deaf to the call of God in His direct "eternal word."

Such, too, are those hopelessly indifferent aesthetes, who slip between our fingers like eels, and can never definitely be grasped, because they affirm all values only as spectators divorced from any consequences for themselves, who are harder to convert than actual haters of God rising against Him in impotent resentment.

For the man formed by the Liturgy, the pure affirmation of that which has value is organically followed by the longing for union with it, and the confrontation of his self with the world of God, present in the value; this affirmation is followed by the understanding of God's call, by the sense of one's own unworthiness, by the asking of God's help and the desire to be transformed. And all this has as its final aim the glorification of God.

However, the decisive feature of true personality is not only the fundamental response-to-value attitude, the living consciousness of the fact that an adequate answer is due to every value, the sense of the objective disharmony implied in every non-response to value. True personality also demands a clear understanding of the *hierarchy of values,* the preponderance to be given in the response to the greater value, and leaving behind what is less important. In this inner conformity to the objective order of values lies the secret of true personality. Pettiness, limitation, stupidity, consist precisely in failing to grasp the difference between higher and lower values, between the essential and the less essential; they consist in clinging to the less important and in giving up the more important; the renunciation of his birth-right by Esau for a mess of pottage; the incapacity of renouncing the lesser value for the greater one and abandoning something unimportant in favor of a higher value because the unimportant is so habitual and familiar that it seems impossible to give it up. The great, free personality manifests itself precisely in the fact that like the merchant in the parable of the Gospel he sells everything in order to acquire the single pearl of great price; he freely abandons the habitual and familiar in the name of a higher value, clearly realizes the hierarchy of values, and does not confuse the habitual and the weight implied in the height of the value.

But it is not sufficient that a person should give his preference to the higher value in his action only, in placing foremost only the higher moral demand.

His entire attitude towards the world of values must take this hierarchy into account.   The admiration and veneration which he offers a value must correspond to its objective height and so, too, the joy which he feels about something, the place he reserves for a good in his soul.   Of what worth is it for a man to be enthusiastic over a master-piece of art if at the same time he admires as much an insignificant work?   Of what worth is it for a person to be enthusiastic about a saint if in the same breath he praises to the same degree an ordinarily meritorious and deserving man?   This defective gradation in the order of response de-substantializes the affirmation of the value.   If everything is placed in the same scale, even the greatest enthusiasm over a true value is but a fire made of straw.   In placing everything on the same scale, such men remain empty even when they are closely in touch with the world of values.   These values do not clothe them with their nobility, and they slip off without filling them with their spirit.

True perception of value implies the clear grasping of the hierarchy of values.   The awareness that a response is due to the value implies necessarily that the response must be an adequate one, and that

a higher value demands a response *different* from
that which is due to a lower value; it therefore means
that the gradation of values is also required on the
part of the person.   The more inner room a person
reserves for the higher values, without letting himself be submerged by the less important ones, and
the more he can inwardly dispose of a new register
when the higher values arise before his spiritual eye,
so much the more is he a genuine *personality*.   This
is true not only of the attitude towards the values
as such, but also of the attitude towards objective
goods enjoyed by the person — freedom, health, liberation from concern about everyday life, respect on
the part of fellow-men, success in professional work,
contact with beauty in nature and art, friendship,
marriage, in so far as they mean for us a gift of God
and bestow happiness on us.   Here also our suscep-
tibility to a certain good, our longing to possess it,
must be submitted to a gradation according to the
degree of the value implied by the good in question,
and the corresponding nobleness and depth of its
capacity to dispense happiness.

It is above all a sign of deficiency in depth and
breadth when a man thinks more of goods which

merely procure pleasure, such as good food and drink, the comforts of life, ownership as such, than of goods providing spiritual happiness such as a deeper penetration into truth, contact with the deeper world of beauty in nature and art or a noble communion. When we speak of materialistic men as opposed to *spiritual*, men spreading an oppressive and narrowing atmosphere even when they are men of good will from the moral point of view, we mean precisely those whose receptiveness for pleasure-dispensing goods is greater than receptiveness for happiness-dispensing goods.

But the maintenance of an objective gradation in our attitude towards happiness-dispensing goods is also of decisive significance for the depth and greatness of personality. Limited, indeed, is the man who places his professional work as such, the usual development of his faculties as organizer in a factory or a political party, above the gift of a deep communion of love, he whose soul is more liable to be filled by this and inwardly more attached to it. For of all created goods, the true communion of love with another human being is the highest and noblest one of all, as it is expressed in the words of the Canticle of Canticles: "If a man should give all the substance of his house for love, he shall despise it as nothing."

"The greater the man, the deeper his love," says Leonardo da Vinci. According to the kind of happiness he thirsts for, the greatness of a man can be recognized. The goods that attract a man and polarize his tensions also determine whether he is a personality in the true sense of the word. The greatness, depth and breadth of a man is revealed by the diminishing receptivity for all minor things which recede and even vanish before some major gift granted to him by God. Take the case of a man who beholds some new world of sublime transfigured beauty, as for instance in seeing Italy the blessed land of redeemed beauty. If his interests in trivial goods, in familiar comforts, sports, amusements, is not immediately silenced and blunted, that man is a narrow individual. Again, a man receives the great gift of discovering another person who has a mysterious affinity with him; he fully understands the essential secret logos of that person and feels his own secret word understood by him so that they can become one in Jesus. Suppose that in spite of all this he does not spontaneously put aside and suppress his clinging to the familiar goods of life, is not inclined to sacrifice his "smugness," comfort and even the reputation of a reasonable man which he enjoys in the eyes of his fellow citizens. Suppose he is not ready to give up "all his possessions" and to consider them as naught. Such a man is not a personality in the true sense of the word.

Yes, he only is a true personality whose thirst for happiness cannot be satisfied with any created good, and who says with Saint Augustine, "Troubled is our heart until it rests in Thee."

The ultimate criterion of true personality is implied in the longing for God as the highest good, in the *Quaesivi Vultum tuum, Domine,* in becoming aware of the inner room, which God alone can fill, in the spontaneous withdrawing from and putting aside of all other ties even with real goods when a ray from God's face falls on us, when God's finger touches our soul, and when we are ready to sell everything in order to acquire that unique pearl of the Divine Kingdom. This is the summit of all conformity to the objective gradation of values and goods for the person. Only he who possesses the right sense of this gradation and takes it into account in his joys and enthusiasms, desires and conduct, renunciations, receptivity and clingings, possesses that spirit of inner freedom and breadth, unlimitedness and dimension of greatness which characterize true personality. And only he, moreover, is free from satiety and stagnation in blind alleys; only in him lives that longing to approach God ever closer which lends wings to man's whole being, discloses to him the knowledge of the cosmos and, above all, leads him to seek and find in all values God's face. This longing is a pre-condition of true communion with Christ and through Christ with the Holy Trinity. It is the longing of which Saint Bonaventura speaks at the beginning of the *Itinerarium mentis in Deum:* "These things can only be understood by him who like Daniel is a man of longing."

In the Liturgy we find this *sense of value-gradation* reflected in a unique fashion. Its fundamental gesture of giving God the preponderant place in us is the most important expression of this sense of value-gradation. The liturgical act itself means to begin with the putting in its right place of the "only necessary thing." In the early morning when the "world" is asleep, the glorification of God begins in the Matins. This is not a hurried glance cast on God in a frame of mind already burdened with the tension of the day's work and the expectation of what the day may bring for us and our interests. It is a dwelling before God in a broad expansive rhythm, *Domine, labia me aperies et os meum annuntiabit laudem tuam* (O Lord, Thou wilt open my lips: and my mouth shall declare Thy praise), a putting forward of that which is most important, of the *opus Dei* which is urgent above all else, the praise and glorification of the Only One *ex quo omnia, per quem omnia, in quo omnia sunt* (from Whom are all things, by Whom are all things, in Whom are all things). It is a contemplative abiding before the *magnalia Dei* and the message of God addressed to us in the lessons. After the *Te Deum* in which in praising, thanksgiving, and petitioning we traverse the entire contents of revelation, a new stream of divine praise and glorification begins in the Lauds; it is only in Prime that a glance is cast on the day which is beginning and the work it has in store for us, its joys and sorrows; it is the placing of the day before God with the prayer: *Dignare,*

Domine, die isto sine peccato nos custodire (Vouch-
safe, O Lord, this day to keep us without sin); *Et sit
splendor Domini Dei nostri super nos, et opera
manuum dirige super nos, et opus manuum nos-
trarum dirige* (And let the brightness of the Lord
our God be upon us, and direct thou the works of
our hands over us; yea, the work of our hands do
thou direct).

The very breadth with which the *coram ipso*, this
"standing before Him" embedded in the prayer of
Christ, is performed in preference to all other things,
is a clear manifestation of the truth of the Benedictine motto, "Nothing must be placed before divine
service" (*Operi Dei nil praeponatur*). In this is
expressed a classical formula for the clear awareness of the true gradation of values.

The penetration of the true gradation of values is
even more clearly expressed in the Holy Sacrifice
which we offer God through Christ, with Christ and
in Christ. Before all else must be offered to God
the highest, the only adequate adoration and gift:
His only begotten son, Jesus Christ Himself. The
only eternal Word which God has spoken and speaks
eternally, which He has spoken to us in the Incarna-

tion, we now are allowed to "speak" to Him, and
then to receive Him, our Resurrection and Life.
We can even now embrace the "longing of the eternal hills," and be mysteriously absorbed in Him in
Whom "the entire plenitude of Godhead is." Again
and again during the day, we emerge from the stream
of life and out of all that holds us in a state of movement and tension in order to turn to the eternally
Same, unchanging, infinitely glorious and holy One,
infinitely deserving of love. This rhythm of the
Liturgy is the strongest expression of the true hierarchy of values.

In the articulation also of the Liturgy, and in the
structure of the liturgical year, we find expressed in
a unique fashion the spirit which demands that the
true hierarchy of values should be taken into account.
Let us recall the complete and precise gradation of
feasts: doubles of the first class with a privileged
Octave of the first order like Easter, the feast of
feasts, and Pentecost; doubles of the first class with
a privileged Octave of the second order like the
Epiphany and *Corpus Christi;* doubles of the first
class with a privileged Octave of the third order like
Christmas and Ascension; doubles of the first class

with an ordinary Octave like the Assumption, All Saints Day, the feast of Saint John the Baptist; doubles of the second class like the feasts of the Apostles; greater doubles like the feasts of Mary Magdalene and the founders of great orders; ordinary doubles like the more important feasts of saints; semi-doubles, and single feasts. The rank of the feast corresponds to the objective scale of the mystery of each feast, and this implies the inner melody which fills the entire Liturgy of the day, the degree of resplendence, joy, glorification, the weight of the celebration, the entire "expenditure" of festivity and rejoicing.

All this is expressed plastically in the fact that certain parts of the Liturgy appear only in connection with a certain degree of festivity as the *Credo* in the Mass, the *Te Deum* in Matins, as the Alleluia and its variations, a sequence in the greatest feasts, and the proper Prefaces. Further, this spirit is reflected in the thought-content of the individual texts of various feasts as in the *haec dies quam fecit Dominus* of Easter, and in the often repeated *"Hodie"* of Christmas. Again, we find this spirit in the atmosphere of the entire linguistic expression, the width and breadth of the feast's celebration, in its being preceded by a vigil in which its light is projected, and its prolongation by an Octave.   And we also find it in the fact that all other feasts are displaced because of the greatness and resplendence of the feast in question as expressed in the degree of exclusiveness of an Octave; all this moreover is reflected in the modes of the plain chant, the celebration of High-Mass with deacons and subdeacons and incense and even in the outward decorations required by the feast, the display of candles, and so on.   The hierarchy of values is also expressed in the fact that a secondary feast is preceded by the greater feast and makes way for it.   It is the achievement of what we have defined above as the sign of true personality: the lesser value inwardly "makes way" for the greater value.

People who are not familiar with the spirit of the Liturgy think that this precise gradation of feasts, the exact regulations governing what feast takes precedence over another, are but a form of juridical pedantry which should have no place in the religious sphere.   But those who penetrate deeper will recognize that a great and central principle is here exemplified, a principle which should also bear on the attitude towards the cosmos in the life of the individual so that his life should really be in tune with the objective logos of being.

VII

THE STATE OF BEING SPIRITUALLY AWAKE IN THE LITURGY

One of the deepest marks of true personality is the state of being spiritually awake. A genuine personality is distinguished precisely from the average man by the fact that he does not wade through life in a state of spiritual inertia; that he does not contemplate in an isolated way what approaches him but beholds it in the light of the general cosmic background, *in conspectu Dei*, and lives in the metaphysical situation of man. This does not mean being awake outwardly, a certain alertness possessed by practically minded people, and often found wanting in the spiritually gifted, a quick grasping and understanding of outward conditions, a certain preparedness and mental dexterity. This quality, so characteristic of practical people, may coincide with the absence of being inwardly awake which we here have in mind. On the contrary, this state of being inwardly awake is sometimes possessed to a high degree by people who are readily absent-minded, act distractedly, fail to grasp conditions and circumstances where practical business is concerned, lack a certain clearness, precision and quickness of mind, and are therefore mocked at by practical people and regarded as dreamers.

This state of being inwardly awake means turning our face spiritually towards the sphere of values, keeping oneself open to their irradiation, a preparedness to go along with them spiritually, to "*conspire*" with their meaning and content, to conform to the *sursum corda*, the "let us lift our hearts," which the values address to us, and to let oneself be exalted by them. Many people are not blind to values, but they leave it to chance whether or not a value reveals itself and seizes them; they let themselves "drift" and be carried wherever the stream of circumstance directs their impulses and fleeting moods; they abandon themselves to the law of inertia of their nature; their life is a perpetual "letting-oneself go," and hence a life on the periphery. They are spiritually asleep even when they are men of good character and good will. They allow themselves to be completely dominated by circumstances, and one day follows the other without their being "awakened" to a deeper insight into the world and themselves, without questioning the meaning of being and of themselves.   In the spontaneous perception of all things, in practical dealing and management, they live without ever experiencing "wonder" at being and its mysteries.   However talented and gifted, such "un-awake" men are not personalities.   They do not really "live" their lives but let themselves, so to speak, undergo their lives.

There exist two dimensions of being awake.   One is the attitude in which the depth of things is open to the person, an inner readiness to fully receive and penetrate the essential beheld by our spiritual eyes. The other is the awareness of the general situation of being in all that one experiences, the consideration of all things against this ultimate background and finally in the light of God; it is the bearing in mind of the fundamental truths once grasped, and first of all the truth of the metaphysical situation of man. The roots of these two dimensions are inter-twined and represent two ways of unfolding of the one fundamental attitude of being awake.   In certain persons, one of these ways may be more developed than the other. Yet both dimensions belong to true personality.

In this sphere there are different *degrees* of the state of being awake towards the true nature of the world. The first degree is the general inclination towards the realm of values and their content of meaning. This distinguishes the "awake" from the obtuse man. Obtuse people ignore the deep content of all the spheres of life, they see only the obvious which needs no spiritual *élan* in order to be grasped; when they grasp a value, they hold it at a "reasonable distance," without letting their hearts be inflamed by its glow. The man who on the contrary possesses the first degree of being "awake" penetrates many spheres of life, the beauty of nature and art, the earnestness and dignity of knowledge, the charm of the world of vital values, and he penetrates them with great intensity. Life in its many-colored and multiform aspects speaks loudly and clearly to him. He lives a full life in a state of openness, readiness and deep spiritual receptiveness. According to the depth of his gifts, this man's awakeness may present various dimensions until it reaches the awakeness of a great genius.

A second degree is formed by the awakeness to moral consciousness: the understanding of the inflexible earnestness of the demands of the sphere of moral values which address themselves to us without asking us what pleases us; the shining forth of the metaphysical situation of man, the discovery of our own power to say to all that arises before us a free "yes" or "no" according to whether or not it is an objective value. A man may possess a certain awakeness regarding many spheres of life and being, and yet not have reached moral maturity and consciousness. Supported by great gifts and talents, he may resist spiritual inertia and be ready to follow the values spiritually; the surrounding world may also speak to him in strong and direct language; free from all conventional de-substantialization, he may be aware of the colorful originality and full-blooded contents of things; his life may be full of intensity and inner content. Yet such a man may not be awake to the understanding of the world of values in its majesty and intrinsic dignity. He has not yet grasped the fact that a response is "due" to values; he has not yet understood that the domain of values is beyond our pleasure and the fortuitous inclinations of our nature. He has not yet discovered his own *freedom*, that freedom which allows us to rise above the inclinations of our nature, to follow the lead of values and turn away from non-values independently of the whims of our temperament; the freedom which grants us the possibility of *sanctioning* or disavowing our impulses, *accepting* or *refusing* an offer made by life. An entirely new and decisive degree of awakeness is implied in this moral consciousness which awakes a man to a fundamentally new understanding of the sphere of values and makes him find "himself" in the awakeness to his own freedom, allowing him to grasp the fact that only the conscious, expressly sanctioned response-to-value satisfies the demand of the realm of values.

As one easily perceives, this moral maturity is an indispensable foundation of personality. In so far as the central point is concerned, without it man remains an infantile being who cannot ripen into spiritual maturity. In spite of its fullness and vitality a man's life without this maturity is plunged in "slumber," in the deeper sense of the word.

A third degree of being awake is the inner openness to God, the harkening to God's voice and to the call of God. This religious awakeness means the inner readiness to let oneself enter into the world of God's mysteries, the state of "keeping oneself open" to the world of God hidden from our natural sight, the state of the patriarchs of the Old Testament, for example, which is also found in Saint John the Baptist, the apostles and disciples following the call of Christ, and in all who have "ears to hear" when God speaks.

This deepest form of awakeness, this opening of the deepest spiritual "organ" for the reception of God's voice in creation, and above all for the grasping of God's supernatural revelation, is more than the pre-condition of faith. It is, in the exaltation of grace, an essential element of the true relationship with God even for him who has found God and is supernaturally bound to Him through Christ and His Church. It is the foundation for a deeper penetration into the truth of faith, the radiation of Divine light in our souls, the grasping of the invitation of grace in us, true prayer, the inner cooperation with Christ when the Holy Ghost acts mysteriously in us. This is the degree of awakeness which alone makes of man a true personality, for this awakeness is first of all an indispensable pre-condition within us for the transformation into Christ and, secondly, part of the resemblance to Christ. There are people fortunate enough to possess faith but not awake, spiritually and intellectually inert people who lack the inner readiness and tension and live in a relative obtuseness. Their being cannot be truly transformed by the supernatural. They have not opened their "organs" in order to let the life of grace stream into them; they keep the supernatural life bestowed upon them by baptism "bottled up" in them.

True awakeness implies receptiveness to God's voice, both inner readiness for the Lord and knowledge of ourselves. "Who art thou and who am I?" Such is the question of the person who is awake. *Noverim te, noverim me* (Could I but know thee, could I but know myself); such is the longing call of one who is awake. It implies the grasping of the true situation of our own self before God, the confrontation previously described of our own self with God. It is an inner self-opening, allowing oneself to be irradiated by the light of God in order to know and find oneself in this light.

Here we find the two dimensions of awakeness

previously mentioned. We find this ultimate let-
ting-oneself-remain-open, this readiness and receptiveness spoken of by Christ in the parable of the
wise and foolish virgins, the vigil of the Advent of
the Lord of which we know "neither the day, nor the
hour." This vigil forbids us to live at our leisure,
to let ourselves go peripherally to the impulses of
our fallen nature in such a way that our ears become
obdurate and no longer hear what God says to us
and we "slumber" when the Lord calls us. But we
also find the other dimension — the life, *in conspectu Dei*, constantly keeping in mind the true situation in which we live. This awakeness forbids us to
be so absorbed by certain goods as to forget God the
"first truth"; it prevents us from living so intensely
in the visible world which surrounds us as to forget
what stands behind and above that world and in
whose light alone all that which belongs to the visible
world acquires its genuine visage. It is the awakeness whereby we do not allow ourselves to be absorbed by what is at hand, by urgent business and the
day's work keeps us centered on God, His Kingdom,
our vocation and the supernatural meaning of our
lives. In one word, it is the awakeness which is a

dwelling in the presence of God, an abiding in His light. Both dimensions are inter-linked. The more we live with our gaze fixed on God, abide in the consciousness of this only true world and our own fundamental situation and see everything in that light, the more are we open and receptive, the more does the deep content of all that falls under our spiritual eyes speak to us and the more acute is our ear for hearing the voice of God. From this awakeness organically flows also the knowledge of the dangers threatening our ultimate vocation and the need to watch over temptations. This awareness of dangers however does not constitute the entire content of true awakeness but is merely part of it.

It is to both these forms of being awake that the Lord urges us with extraordinary force in the Gospels: "Watch ye therefore, because you know not the day nor the hour when the Lord cometh"; "Behold, watch and pray!"; "And what I say to you, I say to all: watch!"; "Be you then also ready"; "Watch ye, and pray that ye enter not into temptation."

There are few attitudes to which the Lord urges us with so much insistence as to that of awakeness. The apostles do likewise: "But be thou vigilant"; and, "Let us not sleep as others do, but let us watch," says Saint Paul; "Be prudent therefore, and watch in prayers," says Saint Peter; "Blessed is he that watcheth" says Saint John in the Apocalypse.

The Liturgy is pervaded with this spirit of awakeness. The Liturgy is a vigil in itself in the highest sense of the word and organically draws all who live in it into this spirit. In liturgical prayer, we emerge from the grip of our interests and worries, the tension centered on our labors, the immediate goals of practical life, the importunate "mincing" of being which the visible world offers; we emerge towards the great things that are eternally and invariably important, towards the *mysterium Divinitatis*, the *mysterium Trinitatis*, the *mysterium Incarnationis*, the *mysterium misericordiae et caritatis*, the *magnalia Dei*, the great deeds of God, the mystery of the Suffering Christ and the Eucharist. We emerge from the visible, not just to cast a fleeting glance on that world of mysteries, but to abide in it at length, believing, hoping, loving, thanking, praying, asking. All this, is the *expressed accomplishment* of awakeness. We sacrifice and pray during the Hours of

the day, not in order to become awake but in order
to *glorify God*. Yet this deep, broad stream of liturgical prayer before God is the actualization of being awake. Participation in the prayer of Christ
means to be awake in the highest sense of the word.
The performing of the Liturgy means also being
awake to ourselves and our true metaphysical situation. Thanks to the Liturgy, we stand consciously
where we objectively stand in truth. Here the card-
board houses of pride collapse; all the illusions of
concupiscence, all repression, all flight from God
and from oneself, all the self-beguilement which is
implied in turning away from true reality, all of this
falls to pieces. Our sin, our guilt, our responsibility, death, which none of us can escape, the danger
of eternal damnation, our nothingness before God,
God's infinite mercy, our redemption through the
blood of Christ, all stand revealed before us. In
the Liturgy which we perform through, with, and in
Christ, who is eternal Truth, we are *placed into
Truth*. All semblance and twilight are dispelled
through the *Lumen Christi;* all is laid bare in that
light — ourselves, our condition, our vocation.

All earthly goods, our earthly actions and designs,

are also placed in their right place *in conspectu Dei.*
To be awake is not only extended to eternal things
but also to transient and earthly ones. The Liturgy
is in itself awakeness in the highest sense of the word,
and it leads, moreover, all who live in it to being
awake.

Throughout the course of the day with its
"Hours," through a continually renewed "treading
before God," the man threatened with being drawn
into the turmoil of life is again lifted upwards
toward awakeness. Where do we feel more deeply
the consequences of original sin than in our bluntness and thoughtlessness? We know that in so far
as we are baptized, the life of Christ pulsates in us,
that the most Holy Trinity dwells in us, but how often
in the course of the day do we live in that consciousness? We know that Christ stands before us in our
fellow men, but how many people do we actually behold in that light? We know that "only one thing
is necessary," but we trouble about many things.
When a ray of God's glory touches our soul and our
heart is overfilled, how long does this condition last
before we drop back into the periphery and are absorbed by trifles? God may grant us a great gift,

He may let us discover a human being whom we understand ultimately and who likewise understands us, a human being whom we may love with Jesus and in Jesus, in whom we may grasp the unduplicable design of God which he represents, towards whom we have an ultimate mission, and who has an ultimate mission towards us. Yet how soon do we grow accustomed to this gift, how soon does God's kindness become something habitual in our eyes, how soon, in our inertia, do we grow deaf to the call of God implied in the gift, and let it be carried away in the whirlpool of the commonplace? What bluntness in marriage, in friendship, in our relations with children! What bluntness towards all the goods which God's bounteousness bestows on us, towards the beauty of nature, the splendour of truth, health, freedom! For how much of all this do we thank God? How soon does that for which we longed, as for something rare and precious, grow commonplace in our eyes!

We can measure our bluntness by comparison with the confessions of a Saint Augustine or by contemplating a Saint Francis of Assisi. Here is awakeness, the victory over all routine and bluntness, here is a beholding of all things *in conspectu Dei,* a harkening to the voice of God which speaks to us in all goods and providential gifts! Here is a true perception of God's most generous bounteousness, enthralling suavity, a true understanding of all things in their original significance which embodies God's creative design for them. The Liturgy with-draws us from this daily process of becoming blunted, it lifts us out of spiritual slumber, the ob-tuse "taking things for granted," being dazzled by the new only because it is new. The Liturgy frees us from all this by letting us emerge at certain in-tervals of the day into the light of God and actualiz-ing our awakeness in the endless praise, thanksgiv-ing and prayer. But one might ask: is the Liturgy the only way to awake us? Do not the many brief glances we lift to God in the course of the day, mark-ing thus our perception of our true situation, indicate a sufficient form of being awake? Is it not enough, before each task, joy or sorrow, to perform an act of good intention and link all to God?

Without underrating the value of the brief up-ward glance and good intention, they can never re-place the formation in awakeness granted by the

Liturgy. First of all, they lack the organic character of the latter. The Liturgy, as it has previously
been pointed out, is not performed in order to become awake, but only because we owe God adoration, glorification and thanksgiving, and because we
must ask Him to grant us what we need for our salvation. It is not a means for becoming awake; indeed it is itself the highest form of awakeness. In
this lies, as we have already seen, the highest and
most organic mode of inner transformation; we become awake *in* the Liturgy, not *through* the Liturgy.
Furthermore, the Liturgy does not consist in forced
glances lifted upwards at certain moments of the
day; it is organically linked with the rhythm of the
day, with the situation in which each of us is placed
independently of his choosing. Finally, it is not a
mere rapid glance but a prolonged "abiding" before
God, a "standing before him" for a long while. It
is not a forced, punctual act of emerging, but an organic unfolding before God. The rhythm of repose,
and the granting to ourselves of all the necessary time
inherent in the Liturgy, lead us along quite a different path into the world of God, liberate us far
more organically and efficaciously from the tensions

caused by the earthly rhythm of everyday business.

The meaning of the upward glance is an emerging from tentions; through it we should cease to cling to immediate aims, to what must be "accomplished directly," and we enter into the presence of that which is alone important, the eternally essential. It should be a brief irruption of the contemplative attitude in the face of the practical. But these brief upward glances too often also become a "means" which we use hurriedly, still absorbed by the cramped attitude of practical life, and only in order to be able to return with an eased conscience to the turmoil of work. The brief upward glances are not superfluous. They are necessary and even indispensable for the state of being awake. But they cannot replace what is implied here by the Liturgy. They are in their right place only against the background of the Liturgy and growing out of it organically.

Secondly, and this is even more important, liturgical prayer means emerging from the narrowness of one's own life and rejoining the life of Christ and the universal sphere of the praying Church. It is an immersion into the world of God. The man who is only bound to God by brief upward glances and good intentions remains fixed in his own life; he moves in a religious atmosphere which corresponds to his own subjective narrowness; he lives on an image of God and Christ which he has formed by himself. Often, for him, God plays the part of a formidable ruler dominating his life to Whom he must pray to obtain what he longs for, to Whom he formally links everything, to Whom he must after all offer up everything; but He is a God in Whose presence one does not linger, Whose rays do not irradiate one, to Whom one does not give oneself up in pure response-to-value. Such men may also be pious and full of good will; for them too, God is a final end; but they draw God into *their* lives and see Him through the glasses of their own narrowness; they have lost the sense of true proportion; the air they breathe daily is too much determined by the narrow scope of their particular life, even though it is embellished with religion. Such men do not actually emerge from their lives in order to meet God; the fundamental rhythm of their existence is not immersion in God's world and the *magnalia Dei*, nor a participation in the adoring and sacrificing love of Christ; they do not let their life flow into the life of

Christ. This danger cannot be sufficiently stressed.

Emergence from the narrowness of our own life and "awaking" to the true world of God are so difficult a task for our fallen nature even after its restoration through membership in the Mystical Body of Christ that the simple good intention and the brief upward glance do not suffice to overcome this difficulty. This latter form of relationship depends on the peculiar capacity of the person, while in the Liturgy we enter into a relationship moulded by God. The fundamental attitude and thought-content of the Liturgy, its form and entire qualitative atmosphere, breathe the spirit of Christ; they plunge us therefore into being awake to the true world of the supernatural.

Here again the merit of good intention should not be diminished; it has its significance but it cannot replace the Liturgy, the way to the state of being genuinely awake. As long as the day is only filled with good intentions, the danger mentioned above is not excluded; furthermore, only the person formed by the Liturgy will be able to realize the good intentions in the right way. Only in the latter case will the intention receive its authentic moulding. Of course, God can bestow awakeness on the man who does not observe the Hours or attend daily Mass. But we do not speak here of what God bestows through extraordinary graces; we speak of the appreciation of the way leading to that aim which has been offered us in the Liturgy.

Not only is the Liturgy in its entirety an awakeness, a "vigilance" in the highest sense of the word, as implied above all in the sacrifice of Holy Mass through which we are drawn into the full reality of the sacrifice of the cross and the presence of the God-Man's act of adoring and atoning love, but the very structure also of the Liturgy is a being awake and a being awakened. The frequent repetition of the *Credo* in the Hours and the numerous masses of the day represent a particular form of "vigilance." We affirm our belief in the entire content of revelation as a response owed to God. We expressly render *account* to the supernatural reality in renewed professions of faith. This implies the achievement of being awake to the reality of the supernatural. Again and again, the latter arises before our spiritual eyes, so easily distracted by the visible world. It is the same with the continually repeated *Gloria Patri*, the

Te Deum of the Matins of feasts; and every morning
the great call resounds, *Hodie, si vocem eius audieri-
tis, nolite obdurare corda vestra* (Today, if you shall
hear his voice, harden not your hearts). Even the
participation of the body in religious worship, such
as the act of genuflexion, the inclination of the head
during the *Gloria,* standing during the reading of the
Gospels, represent an attitude of awakeness, and at
the same time a call to wakefulness. What a confirmation of the full reality of the supernatural is
disclosed in the fact that even in our physical deportment we conduct ourselves towards what is before us
in such a fashion as if it stood visibly in front of our
eyes! This deportment which may appear to many
as a mere outward gesture is a deep expression of
full awakeness through which we touch supernatural
reality. It forces us into the full genuine "standing
face to face." Yes, even this physical deportment
as such is an expression of awakeness and "waken-
ing" as opposed to "slackness." It is an expression
of inner readiness, a "standing before God" which
helps us to awaken from bluntness, inertia, the shutting up of oneself in oneself.

What a deep and noble symbol of watchfulness is revealed in the praise of God in the night when the world "sleeps," in the Matins, and formerly in all the vigils.   Here the "vigil" even becomes an actual theme; as opposed to the sleeping world, this soaring upward to the true reality is expressed in a peculiarly plastic fashion, as reflected in the hymn of Tuesday-matins:

> *Consors paterni luminis,*
> *Lux ipse lucis et dies.*
> *Noctem canendo rumpimus,*
> *Assiste postulantibus.*
>
> . . .
>
> *Expelle somnolentiam,*
> *Ne pigritantes obruat.*

O God from God, and light from light,
Who art Thyself the day.
Our chants shall break the clouds of night,
Be with us while we pray.

. . .

Chase the sloth and drowsiness that bind
The senses with a spell.

The fulfilment of the liturgical year as a whole is also an expression of awakeness and vigilance. Here we find repeated on a larger scale what the liturgical day represents on a smaller one. We watch before God by holding in mind the great fact of Salvation full of unchanging significance, the *magnalia Dei,* and by participating in the sublime rhythm of the liturgical year. The days do not bear the mark of earthly events linked to the life of individuals or such temporal communities as the state or nation; but they are marked with the consciousness of the *magnalia Dei.* The great deeds of God determine the day and the sections of time in the Liturgy. What a state of wakefulness is implied in this! This is indeed a victorious drive, a breakthrough of all the strata of earthly events clustering around us, the misery of individuals and peoples, the entanglements of states and families, as well as the temporal destiny of the Church. It is a drive towards *supernatural* reality.

And, moreover, what an organic form of being awake! During Advent, the Church permits us to participate in the longing of thousands of years, and awakens us in order that we might await the Advent of the Lord: "Brothers, knowing the season that it is now the hour for us to rise from sleep . . . ," the holy Church calls to us at the beginning of Advent. The Gospel of the first Sunday of Advent places the return of Christ clearly before our eyes. The longing is a specific expression of awakeness. The worst form of slumbering, of bluntness, is to be so absorbed in our business of life that we do not even long for God any more. The entirely blunted man is the satiated one, the man who, satisfied with himself and the world, does not ask for "more."

Advent is followed by Christmas and the Epiphany. What a call to awaken we hear each year at this time, as if the event were happening today, as if we were hearing the message for the first time! What a call to awaken resounds in the rejoicing over the birth of Our Lord, the continually repeated *Hodie* of Christmas, the praise and thanksgiving offered to God for the Incarnation of the eternal Word, in the *Ecce advenit Dominator Dominus* (Behold the Lord the Ruler is come), and in the *Surge et illuminare Jerusalem quia venit lumen tuum et gloria Domini super te orta est* (Arise, be enlightened, O Jerusalem: for thy light is come, and the glory of the Lord is risen upon thee), in the *Vidimus stellam eius in Oriente* of the Epiphany. Then comes the time of Lent. It is the time of the great confrontation of ourselves before God, the full awakening to our burden of guilt and the necessity of atonement and penance before God. We are led into that sphere of awaking which is called self-knowledge, the seeing of oneself in the light of God; and at the same time we are introduced into the sphere of the mercy of God which offers us the possibility of atonement, penance and adoption in Christ and through Christ. *Ecce nunc tempus acceptabile, ecce nunc die salutis* (Behold, now is the acceptable time, behold now is the day of salvation), the Church sings on the first Sunday of Lent. Then comes Passion Week in which we awake to the mystery of Christ's suffering; Holy Week in which we are immersed in the mystery of the Eucharist and the death on the Cross; and then the feast of all feasts, the great awaking to the light of the Resurrection, the glory of the resurrected One, the new opening of the doors of Eternity through victory over death: "Oh Death, where is thy sting?" The culminating point of all awakeness is Easter Week and the time of Easter: *Quae sursum sunt quaerite ubi Christus est in dextera Dei sedens, quae sursum sunt sapite, non quae super terram* (Seek the things that are above, where Christ is sitting at the right hand of God, taste the things that are above, not the things that are upon earth). These words of Holy Saturday are the quintessence of awakeness. This time is followed by the Ascension and the nine days of "awaiting" the Holy Ghost. Where do we find a more deeply expressed unfolding of awakeness in the sense of inner preparedness and harkening than in these nine days which we spend with the apostles in the Upper Room? Then comes Pentecost and we awake anew to the mystery of the descent of the Holy Ghost.

Here the state of awakeness expressed in the liturgical year and its sublime rhythm can be grasped. In the liturgical cycle, the Church irradiates our life with the world of the supernatural; it draws us into the cycle of the mysteries of Faith; we breathe the fragrance of Christ; we hear His voice; we live His life. And this is not an haphazard meditation on the mysteries of Faith in which we indulge alone in an artificial act of an intellectual or emotional nature; it is a direct participation in the pulse of the entire Church, a breathing with the Church, a life in the Church.   Each day is marked and shaped by the Liturgy in such a fashion that it draws us of itself into the supernatural reality so that we live our life surrounded by it on all sides.   Each day is so deeply penetrated with this "watch" before God in sacrifice, praise and thanksgiving that we naturally grow more and more awake.   The Liturgy, as it has already been stressed often, is the deepest form of awakeness because its aim is not to awake us but to give the adequate answer to God's majesty and holiness.

The man formed by the Liturgy is the man who is awake in the highest sense of the word.   He is not only inwardly open to hearing the voice of God.   He is not only aware of the ultimate Truth, but he also looks on all earthly goods in their true light.   Far removed from all bluntness, "indifference," stoic insensibility and impassiveness, his awakened eye is open to every created thing in its mystery of the height and its divine meaning.   Let us recall once more the precious and noble character of created things, such as water, for instance, as disclosed in the

blessing of the baptismal water. What a contrast
to all the blunt, immediate conceptions of earthly
goods received from God's paternal hand is found
in the liturgical *Benedicite;* what constantly awakened gratitude: *Oculi omnium in te sperant, Domine, et tu das escam illorum in tempore opportuno.*
(The eyes of all wait upon Thee, O Lord, and Thou
givest them their meat in due season.) *Benedic,
Domine, nos et haec tua dona, quae de tua largitate
sumus sumpturi;* (Bless us, O Lord, and these Thy
gifts which we are about to receive from Thy
bounty). *Agimus tibi gratias omnipotens Deus,
pro universis beneficiis tuis.* (We give Thee thanks
O almighty God, for all Thy mercies.) At the same
time, everything is organically placed into relation
with the supernatural so that our spirit can rejoin
again and again the unique and eternal, the goal of
our hope: *Mensae caelestis participes faciat nos
Rex aeternae gloriae.* (May the King of eternal
glory make us participate in the divine banquet.)

The man formed by the Liturgy also watches, so
to speak, with "a burning lamp in his hand," and
"with girt loins," for the advent of the Lord. His
life is a life of longing, hope, gratitude, solemn emo-

tion, and openness to the mysteries of being. We
see how deeply awakeness is linked with reverence,
as well as with the consciousness that an adequate response is due to value, and with the sense of the right
gradation of value. The awakened man is also conscious of the ultimate tie which binds him to all men
before God; He sees Christ in his fellow-man; he
lives in the truth of the Mystical Body of Christ.
The more awakened a man is in this sense, the more
fully he exists as a person, the more genuinely he
lives, the truer is his life, the more is he a personality in the original sense of the word.

It is particularly important today to stress this
point. In a legitimate reaction against a false consciousness, many have fallen into the cult of a naïve
unconsciousness and a childish unawakeness. This
is falling into Charybdis in order to avoid Scylla.
False consciousness is of course disastrous; it may
adopt a form of spiritual "squinting" at life, a curi-
ous backward-glance cast on our attitudes and actions, in the accomplishment of life in place of an
immersion of ourselves in their actual objects; it
may also lead to an intellectual dissection and analysis of life and ourselves so that we do not see the

forest because of the trees; this is a hypertrophy of the analytical attitude in regard to the longing for a calm possession of being and reposing in it. But the unconscious man is also incomplete; he is an unauthentic half-man. True consciousness, an indispensable element of personality and an essential part of the transformation into Christ, is nothing but *awakeness.* It means emerging from all the mists of the "vital" and the "unconscious" into the light of the Logos, it means being irradiated by the *Lumen Christi.* It also means the ripening toward that full awakeness which we shall actually possess only in Eternity when we shall be flooded by the *Lumen Gloriae,* when we no more see through a mirror in an obscure manner but, face to face, when we no more know in part, but as we have been known. But the motto of this earthly life is, "Watch ye therefore, because you know not the day nor the hour."

VIII

THE SPIRIT OF *DISCRETIO* IN THE LITURGY

Closely linked with the state of being awake and the spirit of the gradations of values, there exists a certain *discretio*.   It is a sense of distinguishing applied to the world-structure.   In the first place, it is the sense of the dramatic rhythm of being, of preparation, ascension, fulfillment, ripeness and decline.   It is the sense of the degrees of the inner development of a given theme, the "now" of its achievement and its decline.   This dramatic rhythm encountered not only in the course of the day with its morning, noon and evening, or in life with its youth, maturity and old age, but also repeated in many particular situations of life, does not always follow the same kind of rhythm in its rise, culminating point and descent.   More precisely, in the highest and most central spheres of being, as for instance in all that concerns the preparation for eternity, this rhythm is an ascension towards an everlasting summit.   This rhythm is found in the conversion of a man, leading him to become a member of the Mystical Body of Christ and reaching its climax in sanctification which never declines.   That which unfolds itself in time implies an inner dramatic character, an inner organic rhythm of development.   Everything requires its own time of inner ripening in order to be genuine and true.   The sense of the law of the inner development of all things, which varies according to the sphere of being, is an element of that *discretio*, of that *discrimination*, which is a mark of personality.

The fading of this sense is one of the most serious signs of decay of the nineteenth and twentieth centuries.   It is closely related to the technicization, instrumentalization, and levelling of our world.   In the eyes of a great number of people, the mechanical world of technique has become the model for all vital situations and all spheres of being.   Men want to reach their goal as soon as possible, and "by the shortest way," as it is reached in building a machine. They want to leave aside all the so-called "superfluous by-work."   This activist, irreverent attitude results in the dying out of the rhythmical law of the being's inner unfolding, especially in the vital, intellectual, and spiritual spheres. Men have ceased to understand what an indispensable function the so-called superfluous *"by-work"* possesses; they have ceased to conspire with the objective logos of things; they want to fabricate things brutally, from the outside, without any sense of the dramatic character of the being's unfolding itself in time. They continually make short-circuits.

The man who is indiscriminate in the sense described above, understands nothing of the inner structure of a relationship of communion, especially of a communion of love such as friendship and marriage. He does not understand the inner degrees which must be scaled organically in the formation of an "I-and-thou communion"; that an inner law must be observed in progressing along the path leading from a reserved attitude towards another person to loving interpenetration. He does not realize the arrival of the moment which marks the passing from the more general "you" to the more intimate "thou"; he does not let himself be guided by the objective *logos* of the relationship, but blindly seeks to skip all the inner degrees of the formation of a deep

relationship.   But he skips them only in an im-
aginary way, for in reality they cannot be skipped.
He will never obtain what can only be obtained after
mounting these degrees, a deep "I-and-thou" communion.   This does not mean that the mounting
of objectively presented degrees always requires the
same amount of time for everyone.   Sometimes the
progress is slow; sometimes it is rapid; sometimes it
is instantly achieved, according to the special character of the persons involved and their objective
affinity to each other.   But the stages must be *objectively passed through* and cannot be skipped.   Indiscriminate persons disclose the innermost secrets
of their hearts, say "thou," behave as if a deep "I-
and-thou" communion already existed, without being aware that they are still objectively in the peripheral attitude of an "outside contact" with the
other person.   Such people do not suspect that *every
word filled with inner content presupposes a fullness
of time* in which alone it can be validly spoken.

Such are the people, too, who believe that one can
"establish" a religious order provided one has in
mind an adequate religious aim, just as one creates
a religious association.   They think that a suitable

plan, a meritorious aim, are also sufficient here in order to call a sacred entity into being. They believe it is quite possible to start a propaganda campaign in favor of their plan, with the aid of books and speeches, and thus to recruit the members of the future community. They do not understand that such a sacred entity must grow silently from within. The founder must not only conceive a good idea but must lead primarily a life dedicated to God. Without planning the creation of a religious order, he simply obeys God's call in leading a life according to evangelical counsel. Then others will crystallize around him and form a life which will later be firmly shaped from within, as was the case with the Benedictine, Franciscan, Dominican and Jesuit orders.

Equally, men lacking the spirit of *discretio* do not realize the stages of listening, receiving, quietude, recollection and silence, which must be observed before an explicit apostolate becomes possible. There are people who immediately after conversion and finding their way into the sanctuary want to act apostolically and redress wrongs instantly. They do not feel how much time is required for listening, silence, prayer, and inner preparation by God, in order that an apostolate might be validly filled with the life of grace, and yield its fruit in the Lord's vineyard.   Here we find the same defective sense of the inner dramatic essence of being, the same in-comprehension of the inner stages which must be traversed before the moment has come to speak the inner word genuinely.

The fading of the sense of *discretio*, which we witness today, is expressed in the smallest things. Many consider that it is a superfluous convention to welcome one's friends expressly before speaking of other things, or to take leave of them; so, too, when it comes to saying "good-morning" and "good-night" to persons who share our home.   They do not grasp the fact that this custom implies a deep meaning — the necessity of rendering account to the inner articulation of a communion-situation. The fact of being together with other men demands objectively that before casting a common glance at the material, before exchanging impressions and experiences, there should be accomplished an act expressly meant for the other person as such, in which the "bi-personal range" is established.   It is

the same with every leave-taking.   To skip and neg-
lect these things is a violence done against the inner
structure of every communion-situation.   The uttered welcome and fare-well imply not only an expression of outward courtesy, as for instance the conventional use of a title, but they also imply a far
deeper dimension.   They imply the fact of taking
the other human being seriously, of giving him full
consideration as a person; it means that one fully
takes into account the inter-personal situation and
its organic structure.   To skip and overlook this
fact, as if it were a superfluous formality, to regard
it as fussy and ceremonious, are typical cases of
the lack of *discretio.*

Along with this incomprehension, we find the lack
of the sense of the inner fullness and scope of certain
moments, of a full "now" in which inner development reaches its culminating point and in which
something portentous attains completion.   It is the
lack of the sense of such moments in our life which
may be compared to what in the evolution of the
world are called "historical moments."   In the eyes
of indiscriminate persons, life flows so uniformly
that they do not grasp the inner solemnity of a mo-

ment charged with meaning; for them, there is no full "now." They have no feeling for the decisive, solemn "now" of such a moment as when a bridge is suddenly established between themselves and another person through a first loving glance. They have no feeling for the "now" of a farewell before a long separation, or a meeting after a long absence; nor do they feel the "now" of a man's birth and death, the "now" of baptism and conversion, a deep crisis or a great decision. With what a deep symbolism were all important moments in which a new phase of life was to begin formerly clothed, a symbolism which stressed the decisive character of the event! Suffice it to recall the ceremonies held when a person was knighted, promoted from the state of apprentice to that of master, received a doctor's degree, or signed a contract.

Compare these ceremonies to the way contracts are signed even by States in the present, not to speak of the unostentatious passing from one professional degree to another. What a levelling of all solemn moments! Is this not a clear sign of the fading of the sense of the full "now"?

The spirit of *discretio* implies secondly the sense

of the strata of depth at which one moves and should move; it is the sense of not mixing up the levels and not passing unaware from one level to the other. Many people, finding themselves in a certain situation, glide from a genuinely religious attitude into the far more peripheral one of a simple profession of their *own* convictions without even noticing this transition. How many slip from a reverent attitude of obedience to God into the sphere of merely correct allegiance and propriety! They slip from the sphere of sincere sorrow into that of self pity. They mix up the superficial emotions caused by childhood memories with true religious emotion. They pass from the deep strata of self-giving to a person in need to the merely sportlike enjoyment of being useful. There are women who pass from the sphere of loving sacrifice to that of the mere satisfaction of their motherly instincts. Though a woman's care for her husband may have been in the beginning an expression of devoted love, it may become imperceptibly a self-satisfaction induced by taking care of someone, or even an occasion for displaying domestic talents. It is not the satisfaction as such which is detrimental to *discretio,* but the fact of not noticing that it is something superficial compared to the genuine, initial, loving sacrifice.   There are men who without being aware of it pass from the sphere of genuine asceticism into that of a self-discipline akin to the training required by athletics.   Others abandon genuine apostolic activity for the task of recruiting members to the "cause" of their own party.

It is a sign of true personality to distinguish the various levels of depth in oneself and not to slip unaware from the depth to the surface in one's attitude to a given good.   Yes, a true personality has such a sense of the different levels in himself that he approaches a good only at the depth suitable to it; he is incapable of speaking of deep things while preserving a peripheral attitude; he feels the inner impossibility of shifting onto the peripheral plane those things which belong to the depths.   The indiscriminate, in this sense of the word, will also fail to distinguish the various strata in other persons; he says things at the wrong moment; he crudely lays bare and forces to the surface things lying in the depths of the other persons.   Such men unsubstantialize many things by speaking in the wrong way

about them, by repeating peripherally things genuinely spoken in the depths. When they are en-
trusted with the innermost secrets of another, they
do not receive this "word" in their own corresponding depth, but let it drop into the periphery of mere
loquacity.

One must not, however, interpret *discretio* as an
apanage of reserved men, as if the uttering of what
lies in the depths were already detrimental to *discretio*, and as if expansive people were always in-
discrete. The question is not whether a person is
reserved or expansive, but whether or not the level
of expression and divulgence corresponds in its
depths to the depths of the experience. Men who
relate their most intimate affairs to everyone, who
confide deep things to unsensitive and uncompre-
hending people, are indiscriminate in our sense of
the word. An adequate divulgence however, an
opening of oneself in a corresponding situation, is
precisely a sign of *discretio*. For it also implies the
utterance of the "word" objectively demanded at the
given moment instead of leaving it in the darkness of silence. The discriminate, in our sense of
the word, understand precisely the necessity of ex-

actly divulging at the right moment what is then thematic.

Finally, this *discretio* implies the sense of gradations in relation with a certain good, especially the
gradations in relation with the Kingdom of God.
This sense is naturally possessed by most people in
respect to certain spheres.   Take, for instance, the
building of a palace, let us say the Palazzo Farnese
in Rome, upon which many artisans and workmen
were employed besides the great artists like Michelangelo and San Gallo.   The gradation in the relations with the essential theme — the realization of a
work of art — should be accessible to all, except the
hopelessly obtuse.   It is obvious that the activity
of the artist is penetrated with the objective logos
of the work of art, while the work of the mason is
only superficially in contact with its spirit.   The
activity of the mason is not in itself qualitatively
stamped with the *logos* of the work in question so
that this activity can be distinguished from the building of an inferior, artistically defective monument,
as for instance the Leipzig war memorial.   In the
building of the Farnese Palace, this activity may
represent quite a different value in so far as it serves

a positive value; while in the case of the Leipzig war memorial it represents a negative value, not in the moral sense of course, but in so far as it contributes to the creation of something having a negative value. It is moreover desirable for the mason to possess artistic understanding and rejoice in the participation of the creation of beauty. His work will then acquire subjectively a new quality through the consciousness of serving a value, and this consciousness will render it more noble. But this does not alter the fact that this form of service to the objective value is far more loosely linked to the good. And the mason must humbly admit that the artist's service is bound to the value by a far deeper and more significant link which is truly congenial.

As we have said above, here the gradation is clearly seen by almost anyone. In certain other spheres, on the contrary, especially in the religious one, many have lost the sense of gradation in the service of the Kingdom of God. Of course, all that we do should be subjectively transformed into service to God. But the objective distinctions which consist in the *kind* of service rendered to the Kingdom of God should not be effaced. We must possess

the clear sense of how far a service, useful in itself
to the reign of God, is objectively stamped with its
seal, how far it is sacred, how much it approaches
the original theme of the reign of God.

Many people have ceased to be aware of the difference in the degree of service between the organiz-
ing of a political party founded on the Catholic conception and an apostolate in behalf of the reign of
God based on preaching and example.   Many people believe that the recruiting of members for a
Catholic association belongs to the same scale as the
preaching of a sermon.   Take for instance the
action, useful in itself, of a distinguished Catholic
scholar in some neutral scientific sphere, exemplify-
ing that there is no contradiction between scientific
creativity and the Catholic faith.   Many will place
this action on the same scale as that of an apostolate
expressed in life-long scholarly work inwardly penetrated and fructified by the spirit of faith and the
Church.   There are even many people who do not
clearly distinguish the keeping in order of parish
files from participation in the Holy Mass.   They no
longer understand the essential difference between
a Catholic association with a sacred aim and a re-

ligious order which is a sacred entity. We often
hear that all this is meant for the glory of God, that
it is all performed in a spirit of good intention, and
that therefore it is all divine service. Of course,
everything can be "consecrated," but this implies
much more than good will. It implies making room
in oneself for the reception of grace and exposing
one's soul to the rays of Christ's visage, the accomplishment of all things not only for God but from
the lived "I-and-thou" communion with Jesus, from
the living membership in the Mystical Body of
Christ, a membership which attains its summit in a
life that has its sources in the Holy Sacrifice of the
Mass. And yet all this does not in any way efface
the degree of the *objectively* given kind of relation,
binding content and activity, to the reign of God; it
does not alter the essence of the service, its degree
of proximity to the mystery which it possesses in
itself because of its own content.

The clear sense of this great scale of "service
rendered to God," rising until it reaches the unique
service in spirit and truth, the offering of the sacrifice with Christ, through Christ and in Christ, is the
indispensable precondition for the consecration of

all activities even if they are indirectly linked to the reign of God.   The man who lacks this spirit, in spite of all his good intentions, will run the risk of beholding the sacred in the light of the profane, the supernatural in the light of the merely natural. He will even attend the Holy Sacrifice of the Mass in an attitude of ordinary loyalty and obedience towards God and the Church; he will not be able to distinguish these from a superficial and indirect service rendered to the reign of God.

This element of *discretio* in the discernment of gradations in relations is also a mark of personality in its true sense; without it there can be no organic contact with the world of values, no formation of man through value, no true transformation into Christ.

In the Liturgy we find the spirit of *discretio* expressed in its three lines of development.   Its structure and atmosphere clearly testify to this spirit, and the man who lives in the Liturgy grows organically into that spirit.

Let us recall the structure of the Holy Mass.   Behold its organic unfolding for participation in the mystery.   It is not a hurried march towards the great final aim, Holy Transubstantiation. One is aware that certain stages must first be passed through. First the *Introibo* mounting with the *Confiteor* to the altar of the Lord, the confrontation with God, the prayer for the forgiveness of sins, and then the centering of the Mass on the mystery of the feast of the day, as expressed in the *Introit*. Then the *Kyrie*, the great solemn cry for mercy; the adoring praise and thanksgiving offered to God in the *Gloria*; the *Oratio* with the special allusion to the mystery of the feast of the day; the illumination and preparation of our spirit through the epistle or the lesson. Then comes the praise of the Gradual and the *Alleluia*, which rise as an echo to the epistle; and then the even more solemn and deep illumination of the words of eternal life of the Gospel. The *Credo* resounds as a solemn response to the revelation contained in the words of the Lord through an expressly professed Faith. All this is an organic preparation, an ascension toward the mystery. Then follows the Offertory in which we give ourselves up to Christ in order to be carried by Him and with Him to the Father; the elevation of the host and the chalice; and the *Lavabo* which is another purifica-

tion on a higher scale, performed alone this time by
the priest directly on the threshold of the mystery.
But we still stand in the world of symbols; it is still
the priest as *representative* of Christ who acts, while
we participate in his act.

As we approach the mystery more closely, we
hear the *sursum corda*. What a deep sense of the
entirely new which is now on the point of beginning,
of the inner elevation of our attitude to a new scale
which is now demanded. But before Christ enters
in our midst to perform the sacrifice of the Cross,
the solemn praise and thanksgiving for the *magnalia
Dei* must resound once more in the Preface culminating the song of praise of the Angels: *Sanctus,
Sanctus, Sanctus!* Now the last veil drops, the authentic *actio* begins, the celebration of the mystery
itself. First, the ultimate, highest unfolding of the
consciousness of communion — the prayer for the
Holy Church and its Head, the loving glance cast
on our fellow men, the drawing of all into the mystery, the glorious vision of the Communion of Saints.
And then, the world of symbols and of human acts
fades away: Christ Himself, our Head, sacrifices
Himself to His heavenly Father.

And, every time, from this highest sacrifice of the love of Christ to His heavenly Father, the blood of atonement streams into this world of suffering and sin; in the plenitude of light of the ineffable glory of this act, all darkness and twilight are once more illumined, and the entire world is drawn into this transfiguration.

Truly we behold in the Holy Mass the primary image of the entire dramatic rhythm of being, all the stages which must be traversed, the necessity of ascension and inner preparation for the utterance of an objectively genuine "Word." In the transubstantiation, we also behold the primal pattern of a full "now." Here we learn to know the moment charged with inner significance; here where time and eternity meet, we understand the ultimate essence of the full "now." But the further development of the Holy Mass is as organic as the ascension to the Holy Mystery. After participating expressly in the sacrifice of Christ, reaching its climax in the prayer *Per ipsum, cum ipso et in ipso* (Through Him, with Him and in Him), follows the third part of the Holy Mass, the sacrificial meal which is solemnly initiated by the *Pater Noster*, the Lord's prayer. In

the first part of the *Pater*, we once more are in the
rhythm intended purely for the praise of God, which
until now has dominated the entire sacrificial act.
In the second part of the *Pater* we ask for the bread
of life and the forgiveness of our sins, which thus
remind us that reciprocal love between men is the
fundamental condition of union with God.   Then
the *Agnus Dei* follows.   We appeal to the mercy
of Christ and ask for that peace which the world
cannot give us, which is however the indispensable condition for the sacrificial meal with Christ.
Through the kiss of peace, we achieve the deepest
preparation of our soul for the reception of Jesus
Christ, the release of all that separates us from
the unfolding of the tie of love which binds us in
Christ.   Then comes the last confrontation with
Christ, *Domine, non sum dignus*.   After this confrontation, the ineffably mysterious, loving turning to us of Christ is accomplished; it is the true
reception of us in Him, the becoming One with Him,
the fulfillment of the highest union of love with Him.

The specific theme of the Holy Mass is now
achieved.   But the Mass does not suddenly break
off here.   The sublime prayers of thanksgiving fol-

low, then the "Communion," a chant of love in which the sacrament of the Eucharist is illumined by the special light of the mystery of the feast. Then comes the post-communion asking for the special grace of the feast as a consequence of the Eucharist for our life and path towards eternity. It is only then that we hear the solemn dismissal: *Ite missa est*, and the *Deo gratias*. And still we linger as there follows the blessing of the priest, for us who are about to depart, and the blessing of the Logos incarnated in the Gospel, in the reading of the first verses of the most mysterious of all Gospels.

We find in the structure of the Holy Mass the primal image of the sense of the dramatic essence of being, its inner laws of development and the necessity of passing through the objectively presented stages. But this sense of dramatic rhythm is also expressed in many distinct elements of the Liturgy, as for instance in the incensing of the altar during the *Kyrie* and the Offertory, the incensing of the Gospel, as well as in the blessing received by the deacon before the reading of the Gospels. We also find it in the purification of the chalice and the ablution of the hands after communion, in the fact that the initial prayers are recited at the foot of the altar, as well as in many other details. These are not mere fortuitous creations of the rubrics, but the expression of the sense of different objective degrees and what must take place in each of these before we dare pass on to the next one. They are the fruit of *discretio*.

We also find this spirit of *discretio* in the structure of the Breviary as well as in the articulation of the various Hours. They are all dominated by the clearly expressed sense of the rise, culminating point and decline, the organic unfolding of a single theme.

This spirit is reflected above all in the rite of baptism and the ritual of Holy Orders. Observe the distinct gradation of the various phases of baptism which in the early ages of Christianity were also separate in time. The very fact that the reception of baptism is preceded by certain exorcisms is a deep and significant fruit of this *discretio,* and we see this first of all in the division of the exorcisms and symbols into three degrees. The first is the degree of the catechumens, the second that of the elect or competent, and the third that of the neophytes properly speaking. They are the three degrees of inner ripening on the path leading to the reception of the sacrament itself. In each degree we find a corresponding exorcism. The separate symbols, acts and prayers within the three degrees reflect in a particular fashion the ever-deepening preparation for the reception of the sacrament. In the first degree there are the threefold blessings, the sign of the cross traced on the brow and heart, the laying on of hands, the salt placed on the catechumen's tongue; in the second degree there are the recitation of the symbol of faith and the *Pater Noster*, both being recited together with the priest who lays the stole on the neophyte, thus introducing him into the Church. In the third degree there are the touching of the ears with the saliva while the priest utters the words: *Epheta* (Open), the casting out of the devil, the anointing with holy oil. Then only follows the actual baptism.

The Liturgy deeply expresses the sense of these various stages which are to be objectively passed through for the achievement of the final aim. This is also reflected in the fact that though today even for the baptism of adults the entire baptismal rite

is compressed in a short space of time, the gradation of the liturgical steps have been preserved
intact.   The neophyte must pass through, though in
a reduced space of time, the various stages of the
path leading to the sacrament of baptism.

The same is true of Holy Orders.   There are
seven different orders still separated in time even
today, organically leading to the essential aim.
What a *discretio* in the gradation of powers required
by the various orders!   How distinctly is there expressed here also that element of *discretio* in which
the degrees of relationship with the Kingdom of God
are clearly distinguished in the various acts directed
towards God.   The divine service of the reading of
the epistle can be performed by one who is still only
a sub-deacon; the divine service of the reading of
the gospel and the preaching of a sermon is open only
to the deacon.   Whereas the latter may distribute
Holy Communion, the priest alone can offer the Holy
Sacrifice of the Mass.

This element of *discretio* was also expressed in
the now extinct regulation concerning catechumens
who were allowed to attend only the fore-part of the
Mass before the sacrifice.   Here we behold a clear

discrimination of the character of the degree of relationship to God, of the stages of sacredness which the different kinds of divine service possess. As long as it was only the word of God which was communicated, as long as the contact with God was established only through *spiritual intention,* the catechumens could remain in Church. But only after baptism were they admitted to participation in the mystery proper in which Christ Himself is present; only then could they take part in the *substantial, ontological contact* with God through the Eucharist. For only through baptism is this ontological link with Christ provided, that link which permits us to actually participate as members in the sacrifice of the Head.

This *discretio* is also clearly reflected in the distinction within the Liturgy between the sacraments and sacramentals. The wholly new degree of sacredness possessed by the sacraments in relation to the sacramentals is clearly expressed throughout the Liturgical treatment. Both are forms of divine service, both are destined to glorify God, yet they are distinctly separate in so far as their objective link with God is concerned. And how deeply is the

entire Liturgy penetrated with the sense of the depth
of the level at which something must be performed.
Its own atmosphere of ultimate depth and of the
presence of God, its profoundly sacred spirit, entirely irradiated by the face of Christ, prevents us
from slipping onto the peripheral level so often
presented by non-liturgical forms of devotion.

Everything in the Liturgy, even the singing, is
formed by the spirit of Christ.   What a world of
ultimate greatness and truth, towering high above all
individual deviations and entanglements, discloses
itself in the solemnly uttered *Deus in adjutorium
meum intende!*   It draws us into the sacred realm
where there is no place for anything profane.

And let us recall, on the other hand, the swamp
of triviality and sentimentality into which certain
modern religious hymns sink even though full of
good and pious intentions.   These hymns actually
invite the faithful to drop into the superficial; they
lead the outsider astray, for instead of offering him
the true face of Christ, as revealed in the Liturgy,
they falsify it through a sugary sentimentality.   Instead of drawing us out of our narrowness into the
pure mysterious atmosphere of the King of Eternal

Glory, instead of revealing to us the entire "suavity," the mysterious splendour of the "fairest of the children of men," they lead us into a world of sentimentality and philistine narrowness repulsive even from the natural point of view. Many hymns induce the faithful to abandon the level of genuine religious emotion for the sphere of childhood memories; or else they incite to a profession of feelings of mere allegiance such as are typical of any Fourth of July gathering. This does not concern the purely aesthetic problem, but rather the question as to whether or not a hymn reflects the spirit of Christ, whether or not it is penetrated with a truly sacred atmosphere; it is the question of the level to which it leads us inwardly when we follow its spirit. Indeed it would be too naïve to believe that the spirit of Christ is always reflected in everything which has been composed with the intention of edifying and is not heretical or immoral.

Let us also recall how many people celebrate Christmas in an atmosphere of pleasant childhood memories, with the burning lights of the Christmas tree, the mutual gifts, and so on. Such an atmosphere may be both *delightful* and charming when it

is free of sentimentality.   But it is removed by a
deep gulf from the sphere of supernatural solemnity
and majesty, from the realm of the mystery of the
Incarnation as marked by the *Invitatorium* psalm of
Christmas Matins.   In the one case we find amiable
harmlessness, in the other we behold adoring reverence before an inscrutable mystery.   In the former
case we run the risk of considering the birth of the
God-Man in a childish or harmless spirit, of trans-
posing a sublime mystery of faith into the sphere of
purely human poetry.   In the latter, we enter the
world of light, "which will shine today."

And what a gulf between the Litany of the most
sacred Heart of Jesus, formed by the spirit of the
Liturgy, and the modern hymns of the Sacred Heart!
In the invocations of the Litany, as well as in the
Office of the Feast of the Sacred Heart, the "mystery
of the Incarnation" and the "mystery of Love" are
revealed: *Cor Jesu in quo habitat omnis plenitudo
divinitatis!; Cor Jesu in quo sunt omnes thesauri
sapientiae et scientiae!; Cor Jesu, de cuius plenitu-
dine omnes nos accepimus* (Heart of Jesus, in
which dwelleth all the fullness of the divinity!; Heart
of Jesus in which are all the riches of wisdom and

knowledge!; Heart of Jesus, of whose fullness we
have all received!). What a sublime, mysterious
world of divine love envelops these words. How
they feed on the mysteries of Revelation! But in the
modern hymns, the heart of Jesus is bared of the
mystery of His divine and human nature in *one* person, and is considered in a purely natural light; it
is not even contemplated in analogy to a natural
generous and magnanimous heart, but to a sentimental, sugary little human heart. Truly, in the
Litany, something of the world of the God-Man is
disclosed to us; but in the modern hymns, this world
is *closed* to our eyes; it is replaced by a world which
is *unworthy* and deviates even from the natural point
of view.

In the piety which is not determined by the Liturgy, the weight is easily shifted to that which is far
less directly linked to God; it is shifted from the
centre to the periphery. For many, attendance at
the month of May devotions or rosary devotions appears as important as attendance at the Holy Mass
on week-days. And even when they do not place
them theoretically on the same scale, they actually
give their preference to the devotions. Yes, many

recite during Mass a prayer of devotion to Saint
Joseph and Saint Anthony.   For many, in the month
of May, devotion to Mary overshadows Easter time.
For them this devotion to Mary stamps the day far
more than does the Easter Cycle.   For many, solemn benediction appears as central as the Mass.
For many, the visit to a famous place of pilgrimage
is a more solemn contact with the supernatural than
that obtained by participating in the Holy Sacrifice.
They tremble in awe far more in touching a relic
than in the Preparation during which we tread before the Lord's altar.   The man who is formed by
the Liturgy possesses, on the contrary, the *discretio*
which makes him aware of the true degrees leading
to the mystery, and also the narrower spheres within
the divine service.   He will fully affirm the venera-
ble non-liturgical forms of piety; he will be fully
aware of their beauty which belongs to them in so
far as they are secondary branches of the primordial,
but he will see and experience them in their right
place where they objectively stand.

The Liturgy teaches us to put everything in its
right place in the realm of God; it bestows on us
that *discretio* in its three dimensions, even regard-

ing the natural order, through which our life becomes real and genuine, and we become true personalities. *A theoretical handling of the Liturgy,*
or the turning of the Liturgy into a topic of research,
will not lead us to this formation. It can be had
only by the true life in the Liturgy, its actual accomplishment, the inner formation of the spirit as
expressed in the monastic Lauds of Monday:

> *Christusque nobis sit cibus*
> *Potusque noster sit fides*
> *Laeti bibamus sobriam ebrietatem Spiritus.*

> (Christ Himself for food be given
> Faith become the cup of heaven
> Out of which the joy is quaff'd
> Of the Spirits sobering draught).

IX

THE SPIRIT OF CONTINUITY IN THE LITURGY

One of the deepest and essential marks of man as a spiritual person is his continuity. This means not only the faculty of remembering the past, of looking back on what we have formerly known and experienced, but also the fact of knowing oneself to be *one* through the stream of time and moments filled with the most varied contents. It means that man possesses not only one stratum of experience, the actual "here and now" which embraces only a limited content, but that he can retain on a deeper super-actual stratum the knowledge of facts, values, and the response to them. Continuity is a pre-supposition for being a full person, the development and abundance of the person, as well as for all responsibility. If a man lived only separate moments without any link between them, if he did not know himself as the same being in the past and present, if all that he experienced, accomplished, and all that was revealed to him, sank back into nothingness before the actual contact with a new "now," he would be only a bundle of disconnected experiences. He would be deprived of the dimension of depth, and he would lack the essential element of personality which is to be an awakened being.

The power of continuity, like freedom, is the mark of every man as a spiritual person, but the degree of its unfolding may be extremely different.

There are unconscious men, always completely absorbed in the present moment. What has happened to them in the past, what moved and filled them, fades away as soon as a new, strong impression takes possession of them. They are capable of feeling these strong impressions, but these are not rooted in them, they do not become their unalterable possession and a background against which new impressions may arise. In extreme cases, their impressions are juxtaposed without order and selection. The present always dominates the past, even when the content of the present is far more insignificant and mediocre. These people glide through life without developing from their contact with values and their experience of joys and sorrows.

When their attention is drawn to their defects, they admit them for the moment but in the next moment everything is engulfed again.   Such men naturally are neither really awake in spite of the force and vivacity of their impressions.   They do not understand in particular that it is not enough to recognize at a given moment a principal truth only to let it be engulfed by a succeeding one.   They do not understand that it is necessary to retain this truth once and for all and to confront with it what arises newly before them.   They fail to understand that each value disclosed to them demands not only a momentary affirmation, but that in addition it demands a *super-actual* affirmation so that it may become a measure for all that life further offers.   In such people the advantage of intensity and power which the present, actual experience possesses over the past turns the scale and not the height of the value and the inner meaning and content of the experience. These men are dominated mostly by "fashion"; what is "in the air" at the present moment in their narrower and larger surroundings conquers them easily.

Besides this type of extreme discontinuity, we find another type of man who is accessible to deep experiences, for whom the truths and values acquired by him have become a durable possession, but who does not resist the onrush of intense new impressions; the inner content accumulated in the past does not serve as a measure for these new impressions. These are the people who do not let what they possess in the depth of their soul become the principle of formation of the present situation. They may love another human being with a great and deep love, and are faithful to that person. But when powerful new impressions invade them, they let themselves be dominated and filled by them; the love which dwells within their depths is "forgotten" as long as the new impression lasts, and this indwelling love does not dominate and form the situation from within. However, if the circumstances appeal once again to their love, when the beloved is once again with them, and nothing draws them into the periphery, the love which lives in their depths comes out again.

The power of the present and the freshness and power of new, unusual experiences exercises too great an influence upon them. They also fail to give to acknowledged values and truths the full response due to them. In their lives, they also do not give a due account to the inalterable essence of truth and the invariable light of values.   The man with a spirit of continuity, on the contrary, maintains super-actually all truths and values.   He observes fully the response-to-value attitude; he possesses a complete understanding of the realm of values and their demands, he fully penetrates them; thus the values he has grasped and maintained become the natural background against which all new impressions stand out; not only do they arise against this background, but also their compatibility with it must be proved. The enchantment and glamour of novelty has as little hold on the man with a sense of continuity as routine has.   The familiar and customary cease to influence him as soon as it is discovered as valueless.   The new, the freshly experienced, will not exercise any attraction on him if it is acknowledged to be without value.   And even if these goods are not valueless, but belong to a sphere of goods which has been "surpassed" objectively by the higher goods he already possesses, he will not be chained down by them in spite of all their actuality.   Just as the lesser value will recede in him of itself before a greater value, even so the new lesser value will have no advantage over the greater value already possessed.

The man without a sense of continuity fails also to understand contrition for wrongs committed in the past and the necessity of expressly revoking a wrong attitude of the past, of asking the forgiveness of those he has wounded, of expressly correcting past errors. He believes that all this belongs *to the past*, if he behaves righteously in the present and commits no more errors, the essential has been achieved. The question of how much a thing belongs to the past or to the present plays an excessive rôle in his life.

The man with the spirit of continuity, on the contrary, understands that the disharmony caused by a wrong or a mistake in regard to fundamental truths does not cease to exist even when the wrong attitude and the error belong to the past.

It is obvious that continuity is an essential trait of true personality. For without full continuity there can be no inner unity of the person, no real growth, abundance, genuine contact with the objective logos, complete union with the realm of values, or the possibility of being innerly stamped with its seal. Without continuity, there is no real communion with persons, real knowledge, faithfulness,

trustworthiness and true happiness. For every real
happiness implies precisely retaining what is hidden
in the depths along with the actuality of the present
moment. In continuity, man already anticipates a
part of eternity. It reflects the situation of eternity,
an eternal "now" in which all is contained, in which
we shall never be parted from the lived, complete
contact with the plenitude of values which is in God,
and in which the response-to-value will never be in-
terrupted. Continuity is moreover a special condition of the transformation into Christ. What is
the use of perceiving the call of God if we do not retain it in such fashion that it becomes the forming
element of our life? If we let ourselves be so dominated by the impressions of the fleeting moment that
Christ does not determine our attitude in life and
does not impress His mark on it, we shall never be
transformed even though our soul is filled with God
as long as we are in Church.

The organic development of divine life within us,
in which we are allowed to participate through baptism, which attains its full personal reality in sanctification, necessarily presupposes continuity. If
Christ must become the "form" of our soul even as

the soul is the "form" of our body, our eyes must be superactually fixed on God. In every moment of our life, Christ must be the corner-stone against which all that is contrary to God must be shattered. He must be the light in which everything is seen and known, the measure which determines whether or not a thing should have a place in our life. Without continuity there is no organic ripening of the person, no up-building, ascension; life remains a perpetual issuing forth, a constant beginning. The man with no sense of continuity denies God the response to His eternal invariableness, the fact that *every moment* belongs to God, that a constant responding-to-value of oneself is due Him, that each content in life must be confronted with God, and that all our attitudes towards creatures and the problems of life must flow organically from this response. Here too, as in awakeness, it is true that the more a man possesses continuity, the more he exists as a person.

Men who lack the spirit of continuity escape our hold, they lack full consistence. We touch their depths at one time, we exchange with them a mutual glance of love, we speak to them a "genuine" word, and they speak it to us; at another time, a stranger stands before us, everything is forgotten, we grasp at the void when we try to take hold of him. Continuity is the foundation of all faithfulness to God, oneself and the human beings whom we love. Without it, there is no true communion. In continuity, the person renders account to the inner unity and consistency of being, and participates in them himself.

The Liturgy, more than anything else, is penetrated with the spirit of continuity, and dispenses this spirit to those who live in it. The daily repetition of the Holy Sacrifice of the Mass and the Hours is a specific expression of continuity, of the sense of the necessity for always sacrificing to God Who contains all values so as to praise and thank Him. The frequent repetitions in the Liturgy, which certain people consider unnecessary and wearisome, testify precisely to this continuity. The *Gloria Patri* must accompany each psalm because our prayer must again and again turn expressly to the mystery of mysteries, the Trinity; the super-actually existent adoration must be actualized anew. Due account is here rendered to God, to what is always equally new, equally significant, ever demanding worship, love, adoration. How often is the *"Deus in adiutorium meum intende!"* repeated! What a spirit of continuity in the eternal actuality of this supplication! How often does the *Confiteor* return! The *Credo* which is so frequently repeated recalls the necessity of continuity. This continually renewed actualization of revelation educates us in continuity. How often is the *Alleluia* repeated, and the *Hodie* of Christmas. In the Liturgy, we are immersed in the realm of Eternity where there is no room for the habitual or sensational novelty. The invariable resplendence of the God of eternal beauty and holiness, the eternally new *suavitas* of the God-Man, is always equally actual, always equally thematic.

Again, what an expression of continuity in the recurrent rhythm of the liturgical year! Every year there is the same unfolding of longing in Advent, the same rejoicing and thanksgiving at Christmas, the same transfigured jubilation at Easter! What a spirit of continuity in the fact that a saint who lived two thousand years ago is venerated today as much as a recently canonized one! In this we see that the same response is eternally due to the *magnalia Dei* in the saints, that we must *maintain* this response, that it must be not only a response uttered once, but an abiding one. The holiness of a martyr who lived eighteen hundred years ago is today as much a motive of joy, thanksgiving and glorification as the holiness of Saint Theresa of the Child Jesus who lived in our time. The gradation of the feasts of saints is determined by the importance of the saint, his rôle in the work of salvation, but never by the time which separates him from us. The always equal actuality of the martyrdom of Saint Stephen, Saint Paul's conversion, the liberation of Saint Peter, which we celebrate each year with an undiminished joy, is a triumphant affirmation of the inalterable significance of all that is a true value. In the Liturgy there truly breathes the spirit of God "for whom a thousand years are as one day." What a continuity in the firmly moulded forms of all the prayers which we constantly repeat! It is not necessary for us to speak new words to God, but only to maintain the objectively adequate, "valid" word in the prayer of the Church and to participate in it always more deeply and originally.

Thus the Liturgy itself is a great actualization of
continuity, a participation in the adoring love of
the Son for His heavenly Father, which always remains the same.   The man who lives in the Liturgy
organically acquires the spirit of continuity; his
relations also will become continuous with all true
values which speak to us of God's glory; likewise his
relations with other men, the community, knowledge,
the world of beauty, nature and art.

Through continuity is achieved the *true simplicity
of the person,* which in spite of all differentiations
manifests ultimate unity because it maintains the
deepest and crowning response-to-value, the response
to God, which forms all the other response-to-value.
In spite of its richness and inexhaustible differentiation, the Liturgy is filled with this simplicity.   The
man formed by the Liturgy is simple because he lives
from God and performs everything in God, because
he performs everything through Christ, with Christ
and in Christ.   For him the fascination of the present moment and novelty, or what happens for the
first time, have lost their power of dispersion.   Over
his life is written *Christus heri, hodie et in saecula,*
(Christ yesterday, today and forever).

X

THE ORGANIC ELEMENT IN THE LITURGY

It is with satisfaction that we frequently encounter in our days a longing for the organic and a repulsion in regard to all that is artificial, superimposed from the outside, arbitrary. Unfortunately, this longing for the organic often leads to certain deviations, such as the divinization of the vital and the distrust of the spiritual component of the human, which are held accountable for the artificial. This longing has lead to the cult of the subconscious and to a disdain for the conscious. All that takes place of itself without the cooperation of freedom is emphasized in man. These deviations are based on a false antithesis of the organic and the inorganic. The true essence of the organic is an all-pervading fullness of meaning. It has two opposites: the mechanical, deprived of meaning; and the artificial, which has a meaning-content, but superimposed from the outside. A mere sum of people is a mechanical structure, deprived of meaning. An association has a content of meaning, but this has been superimposed from the outside, and has given rise to an artificial structure. A family, on the contrary, is an organic structure because it is a community formed from within and originating from what is central in man. A machine possesses a content of meaning, but is an artificial structure. A work of art, on the contrary, is an *organic* structure. The sphere of the mechanical is dominated by the categories of quantity, mere juxtaposition. The sphere of the organic is dominated by the interpenetration of the parts. In the artificial, in spite of the meaning bestowed from the outside, and a kind of interpenetration of the parts, the juxtaposition remains. The more organic a structure, the simpler it is in spite of its differentiation and content of meaning. The more inorganic it is, *the more its simplicity means poverty*.

The living being, the organism, from which the word organic originates, is a typical example of an organic unity built up from an inner centre of meaning; but it is not by far the primary image of the organic. The spiritual person as such is *a unity far more penetrated with meaning* and is dominated by a far greater interpenetration; yet it is truly simple. The spiritual person as a whole is far more contained in his attitudes and acts than the organism in its members and organs. In so far as he is a conscious being, capable of knowledge and inner attitudes, the spiritual person is far more filled with meaning than a mere organism. His contact with being, his capacity to penetrate it, to participate in it spiritually and possess it through knowledge, his conscious touching of value even in the humblest response-to-value belong far more to organic structure than does the brutal causal contact between the living organism and the surrounding world. The spiritual person reaches the summit of the organic, the non-artificial, in the *free* "yes" of the sanctioned response-to-value, in the explicit, comprehending, penetration of value, in the ultimate accomplishment of its inner rhythm. In the sanctioned response-to-value the real giving of self is first reached, for only here does the conscious centre of the person, fully awake, conform itself to the value. The way in which the value touches our spirit, unites itself with it, and engenders the "Yes" of the spirit in us, above all in sanctioned love, is organic in the highest degree, far removed from the mechanical and artificial in the whole natural order.

The world of the artificial presupposes, of course, a spiritual person. In nature, there is only the mechanical and the organic, that which is poor in meaning or filled with meaning from within. Only man as a spiritual person can create a unity of which the meaning has been superimposed from the outside as in the case of all fabricated objects, and especially the machine. But if the spirit is the presupposition of the machine, and if nothing artificial can be produced by life as such, the spirit itself is that which is the most unartificial of all. All the essential, central attitudes of the person are specifically organic, organic too in their meaningful springing into existence, especially in the case of love. But the will also as such is something organic, which responds to a fact possessing a value with a "you shall exist!" A considerable part of what is created by the person is also specifically organic — all the assertions of real knowledge, all genuine works of art and all culture.

Only a relatively restricted realm is inorganic such as the sphere of technique in the broadest sense of the word, civilization, certain community structures as an association, and so forth. Yet this artificial character does not represent something unworthy, but only an inferior value lower in degree in respect to the organic, just as the mechanical in inorganic nature is not unworthy. In its own realm the artificial character is legitimate.

The definite non-value of the artificial begins only at that point where it is introduced into a sphere which is organic in its meaning and essence. Thus, for instance, when we attempt to "produce" extraneously in ourselves a joy which originates spontaneously in a value, or in other words is "generated" through the contact of our spirit with the value. If our will commands an action, this is the adequate way for the springing into existence of the action. But when our will "commands" love instead of seeking only to remove the obstacles which lie in its way, when we command love instead of opening ourselves to the value of the beloved and seeking to approach the person from within in order to allow love to arise in us organically, then our attitude is inorganic. This does not mean however that we must not *desire* to love God and our neighbour.

Our soul, of course, must be constantly filled with this desire, but we must understand the path by which this aim may be truly attained, which is a round-about way. This way is the normal one demanded by the meaning of love. We behave inorganically if in a fit of impatience and over-estimation of our will-power we seek to stimulate love directly, as one stimulates a gesture or an action. The so-called "acts of love," which are "produced" by force are inorganic acts far removed from genuine love which is "generated" in us. We must humbly admit that the greatest and most important function of our will consists in a very indirect preparation of the ground of love. Whenever we betray *discretio* and refuse to obey the inner laws of development, and attempt to "make" something from outside with the help of our will, our attitude is inorganic, artificial in the sense of an explicit negative value.

A specifically typical example of the negative, inorganic attitude is found in that of some women who long for a child before they long for a husband. It is out of the love for the husband that the longing for a child organically arises, as the longing for the highest symbol of the unity of husband and wife. To desire this fruit of the unity of love without this unity itself, shows a lack of *discretio* and reveals the fact that one artificially places foremost an attitude which must organically follow, and not precede, the other one.

The absence of the longing for a child in marriage, the rejoicing even in the fact that one has remained childless in marriage, is also an inorganic attitude, for it breaks off the intrinsic meaningful intention in the mysterious tie between love and the coming of a new human being into the world.

It is a specific mark of true personality that everything is *organically* begotten in the contact of its spirit with values, that its single acts of thanksgiving, praise and glorification grow organically out of this inner plenitude, that its attitude in each situation originates organically from its fundamental attitude, that its ascension and ripening toward sanctification, organically growing out of its fundamental attitude, penetrate all the spheres of the person.

The way to true personality does not lead through the formation of a technique of the will, a decomposition of life into a series of separate, cramped acts, a partitioning of our relations with God into momentary, inorganically linked, quantitatively multiplied little sacrifices, renunciations, appealing glances, intentions. It does not lead through a petty decomposition of God's commandments into innumerable rules dominating every situation in life from the outside. The way to true personality leads rather through the opening of oneself in the depths, the exposing of oneself to the sun of God; it means to be filled with God's glory, the great confrontation with God, and to see and know oneself in the light of God. This path leads through the love inflamed by Christ, through the will inspired by Him, to walk in the ways of the Lord. It implies making room in oneself for the life implanted in us by baptism, giving God the opportunity of speaking in us, watching before the Lord. It means especially the clear understanding that we are impotent to form Christ in our soul *by our own efforts* but that the Lord must transform us; that we cannot save our soul but that Christ alone can save us. It requires prayer for the right thoughts and decisions, prayer for love, the grasping of the fact that our task is only a free cooperation with grace, letting ourselves be transformed by God. The way to acquire true personality is not through the application of a number of pedagogical rules to our own person, a number of acts which are not accomplished for their own sake but only as a means for a determined aim. What is necessary is the growing into God through responses-to-value valid in themselves, demanded as such, and not intended as means.

It is along this path that the *Liturgy leads us.* In opposition to certain forms of extra-liturgical piety, in which transformation is sought through the formation of a technique of the will, the Liturgy unfolds before our spiritual eyes the glory of the Lord. In the experience of the liturgical year, the Liturgy reveals the true face of Christ in its ineffable mysterious beauty; in all its symbols it envelops us with the air of the supernatural; in its chants it immerses us in the atmosphere of a continual Epiphany of the Lord; and in the union of our spirit with that domain, the Liturgy awakens in us holy love and joy, holy longing, and the immovable will to serve God in everything.

In other forms of piety, a military and hence mechanical discipline imposed on life divides the day into innumerable acts of the will and into a succession of emotions. Through a series of separate acts from without having as it were a kind of auto-suggestive character, our life is transformed according to this discipline. The Liturgy, on the contrary, places uppermost the fundamental attitude to God and the enduring being of man; and it is from this fundamental attitude that the separate acts must grow organically. Certain forms of asceticism regard the blossoming of the supernatural as conditioned by a forced mortification of nature, by the application of a stoic indifference to all earthly goods. On the contrary, the Liturgy is organically linked to our nature, and leads us by organic degrees of transformation towards the supernatural. In the Liturgy too, of course, we die with Christ in order to arise with Him; in the Liturgy, too, we die to the world in order to live in God; but this dying is an organic process, it does not mean a killing off and a forced denial of nature, an artificial benumbing, but an inner emptying of oneself for God. This way of linking nature with the supernatural is pre-

cisely typical of the distinction between the organic
and the inorganic path of the transformation into
Christ. An example of this is the attitude towards
suffering in prayer. When a Saint Theresa asked
God for suffering in order to be still more closely
linked with the suffering of Christ, this was an organic consequence of the degree of her communion
with God and the special graces in which she partici-
pated. Her prayer is therefore true, valid, and of a
sublime greatness. But if we wanted to begin our
transformation and our conforming to Christ by asking for suffering, this would be an inorganic, forced
and untrue attitude. This would be to behave as if
we had no nature. The organic way in praying to
God is to ask Him to protect us from sufferings and
ordeals if it please His holy will to do so; but if in
His divine providence God chooses to send us sufferings, we should ask Him to give us the strength
to bear them in the spirit of Christ. Such precisely
are the prayers of the Liturgy.

In the Litany of All Saints on Holy Saturday, we
pray: *A peste, fame et bello libera nos Domine*
(From plague, famine, and war, deliver us, O
Lord); *A fulgure et tempestate libera nos Domine*

(From lightning and tempest, deliver us, O Lord).

In many petitions we ask for the turning away of earthly evils. Thus, for instance, in the prayer of the nineteenth Sunday after Pentecost: "Almighty and merciful God, in Thy goodness put far from us all that may work us harm: that alert alike in mind and body, we may readily devote ourselves to the doing of Thy holy will." Even in the Canon of the Mass, in the prayer after the *Pater Noster*, we pray: *Libera nos, quæsumus, Domine, ab omnibus malis, præteritis, præsentibus, et futuris* (Deliver us, we beseech Thee, O Lord, from all evils, past, present, and to come).

Certain votive masses are also intended to avert earthly evils, as for instance the masses for the sick and for pilgrims and travellers. Along with the petitions to avert evil, other prayers ask for the grace to accept in the right spirit that which is sent by God.

In many forms of piety, which have not originated in the spirit of the Liturgy, the accent is placed on separate elements, and there is an arbitrary isolation of certain religious attitudes, as for instance the ascetic attitude towards the responding-to-value thanksgiving for the goods received from

God, "the Father of all light." The great danger
of being lost in created goods, a danger implied in
our fallen nature, is stressed so much that every
situation in which a created good is granted us is
considered an occasion for asceticism. Thus it is
recommended that we close our eyes before a beautiful landscape and take advantage of this occasion
to offer a sacrifice to God; this attitude is recommended instead of the due response of joy and enthusiasm before God revealing Himself in His creation, of seeking God in this beauty, and inwardly
joining in the objective praise rising from this beauty
towards God.

In other cases, it is recommended that we inquire
on every occasion: "Of what use is this for my
salvation?" This question must naturally be distinguished from the one asked by Saint Aloysius:
Quid hoc ad aeternitatem? (How does this stand in
relation to eternity?), which is a confrontation of all
that is created with God and should help us precisely to see the value possessed by the object in its
true light. The first question implies far more the
consideration of all objects as a mere means of
obtaining eternal salvation, the limitation of our

interests to their usefulness for the task of our salvation. It takes the place of that other attitude in which one first of all rejoices in the value one encounters and affirms the greatness and bounteousness of God revealed in it. The Liturgy knows nothing of this exaggeration and isolation of a religious attitude, justified and good in itself. Everything in the Liturgy is put in its suitable place, everything is seen in the great connectedness of the classical relationship between God and man, everything appears in its organic linkage. Next to the *Domine Deus noster, quam admirabile est nomen tuum* (Lord our God, how admirable is thy name), we find the *Domine, Domine, quis sustinebit* (Lord, who shall stand it); next to the *Gloria,* we find the *Confiteor;* next to the *Rex tremendae maiestatis* (King of dreadful majesty), the *Salva nos fons pietatis* (Fount of pity, save thou me). But this leads to another essential and typical trait of the Liturgy, distinguishing it from all extra-liturgical forms of piety, its classical character.

XI

THE CLASSICAL SPIRIT IN THE LITURGY

He who penetrates the Liturgy with open eyes and heart would like to exclaim, "O Truth, Truth, Truth!" Everything is pervaded here with the breath of the Holy Ghost, everything is irradiated with the *Lumen Christi*, everything testifies to the eternal Logos. All semblance, wavering, illusion, all that is false, extravagant, cramped, are dispelled. The Liturgy is the primal image of all that is *classical* in the highest sense of the word.

The features examined here, the spirit of true communion, reverence, the truth affirmed by the Liturgy that an adequate response is due to every value, the sense of value-gradation implied in it, the light of awakeness which irradiates it, the spirit of *discretio* and continuity, the deeply organic structure, unfold before our spiritual eyes the deeply classical nature of the Liturgy.

The *discretio* especially, and the organic structure,

are deeply linked to this classical character. It is indeed the essence of the classical to see everything in the place where it objectively belongs, all the dimensions clearly revealed, nothing shifted or concealed, everything unfolded according to its logos and in its organic structure; there is no place in it for extravagance, romantic embellishment, the equivocal. Classicism sees the world in its dimension of depth, its luminous plenitude of value, as a manifestation of God. It implies the absence of bluntness, seeing from without, subjective misinterpretation, pragmatic distortion. In a word, all that is rooted in the sources of classicism responds to the objective logos of being to which it is wholly conformed.

This conformity to the objective logos is also a mark of personality. In the beginning of this work, it was pointed out that in the purely natural order the man with personality is already distinguished from the average man precisely by the fact that the classical human attitudes are achieved in him in their unbroken and undeviated intensity, depth and plenitude. In true personality, the essential dominates the unessential; it does not reveal fortuitous peculiarities, but most clearly expresses that which corresponds to the essence of man and lives in the metaphysical situation of man.

The classical man is preoccupied by genuine problems. He acknowledges the danger of sin, realizes his need of salvation, knows the weakness and frailty of his nature, is filled with the longing for truth, communion, love, feels the insufficiency of that which is created, aspires to the absolute, and is "restless until he rests in God." The unclassical man is absorbed in illusory problems. He suffers from things which originate in a subjective constriction, and is tormented with self-engendered problems. The difference between the classical and the unclassical is reflected even in the sphere of sin, imperfection and error. Every sin, of course, and every deviation from objective value, are unclassical in themselves. But this difference between the classical and the unclassical is repeated analogously in the sphere of error and sin. If the character of the contradiction regarding positive values still reflects a dependence on the objective logos; if negatively the real, central problems are in question, if the stumbling occurs in an objectively frail part of our fallen nature, then even the negative acquires a certain classical character. The more fortuitous, tangential, and eccentric a negative value, the more is it unclassical.

Thus, for instance, materialism is a classical error because it is founded on something which presents an objective difficulty for fallen man, because it is the result of spiritual inertia, of the incapacity for "conspiring" with being. Pragmatism, on the contrary, the theory which reduces truth to utility, is so artificial, so far-fetched, that it must be defined as an unclassical error. Gluttony, impurity, laziness, pride, the craving for power, conceit, hardheartedness, cruelty, are classical sins; they are the antithesis of central values; they are the true opposites of positive values; they are linked to the primal human weaknesses and disorders which have arisen from original sin. To sin out of boredom, sophistication, mere infatuation with the sensational, the feeling of self-importance caused by sin, or because of nerves and hysteria, is specifically unclassical. The cult of idols in its literal sense is a classical sin; the atheism of the enlightened is an unclassical one. Suffering from physical sickness, poverty, unrequited love, separation from the beloved, or the great separation of death, are classical sufferings. Suffering from boredom, self-hatred, one's inferiority complex, the impossibility of giving up self-analysis and falling in love, are specifically unclassical sufferings. This does not mean that unclassical sins are worse than the classical ones. We should not make the mistake of considering the relative classicism of certain sins as a value and lending them the glamor of grandeur and originality. Such a conception would be specifically unclassical. It would be a sign of aestheticism, the typical unclassical attitude.

To begin with, every sin ultimately considered is piteous, ugly, foul, petty, lamentable. Secondly, the criterion as to whether or not something possesses glamor and grandeur is quite unessential when we are concerned with its degree of moral nonvalue, with how much it offends God. Unclassical sins actually are usually the less grave ones.

It is important to understand that people who are burdened with unclassical sins are already warped and de-substantialized in their spiritual powers, and that they must first become spiritually healthy before they can become holy. Being cut off from the objective logos, they are also incapable of offending God as much as those who are healthy, but in a certain sense they are further removed from the saint since they must not only be converted and pass from hostility and bluntness to values to a response to them, but they also must be formally changed and pass from a perverted structure to a normal one, from a formal absence of contact with being to living contact with it, from falseness to genuineness.

Our present age is especially rich in unclassical men, unclassical problems and unclassical conceptions of the cosmos. The tendency to make our nerves responsible for all morally negative wrongs such as irritation, egocentricity, bluntness, instead of imputing them to our own freedom is specifically unclassical. What an extraordinary difference in the contemplation of our defects, and the problem of sin in general, between the confessions of Saint Augustine and certain modern autobiographies or the works of modern psychiatrists and eugenicists, who reduce everything to a question of environment and heredity. What a great classical conception of the cosmos is that of Saint Augustine! But what an unclassical levelling of the world is revealed in the modern conception, what a denial of the essential and the original, of the true features of the world!

It is also unclassical to accent the interest in why a person has spoken, his psychological motives, instead of in what has been said and whether it is true or false. No less unclassical is the widespread attitude in philosophy according to which only immanent criticism is applied to great thinkers instead of the verification of their thoughts from the point of view of objective truth.

What an unclassical modern conception, to take another example, is contained in the so-called new "functionalism" which reduces the cosmos irradiated by values to a mere tissue of aims, to a sum of neutral, immanent laws, excluding the truly thematic contents as an unnecessary, subjective, superstructure, a theory which sees the cosmos systematically from without.

It is not, however, only the distorted, unauthentic man who is unclassical, but also the "hard-boiled" individual, that is, the man who disdains the sphere of knowledge, art, the love of man and woman, as more or less romantic fantasies and luxuries, the man who considers economic and political problems, or problems of civilization, as the only really *serious* things in life. He too lacks the necessary "organs" for the perception of the central sphere of life. He is just as unclassical as the aesthete. A specific case of unclassicism is that of the conventional man, of the bourgeois, whose attitude is exclusively influenced by public opinion, the one who belittles the cosmos and renders everything harmless and de-substantialized, the man who is capable only of tame, conditional attitudes towards all things, the entirely unheroic man who does not want to spoil his relations with anyone and lives by the social image which he enjoys by reason of his reputation.

The classical man is opposed to all these types. He is the spiritually healthy man, the man who stands in full primal relation to all spheres of life, who knows the world in its true dimensions, whose response to values possesses inner plenitude, and is heroically unconditional. He understands that there is something great in the knowledge of truth; he grasps the earnestness implied in a great work of art; he clearly sees the depth of greatness of the love of man and woman, the mystery of the birth of a new human being, the glorification of God in loving communion with Jesus or in a saintly friendship. He sees the great symbols and analogies which penetrate the entire cosmos; he sees, first of all, everything in the light of Christ, in the light of the ultimate truth, in its breadth and depth, in its objective gradation, and his responses are in harmony with this. He is, in other words, and as we have said already, the man who is inwardly conformed to the objective logos.

In the fulfillment of the Liturgy, which breathes more than anything else the spirit of classicism, man is placed in the truth; he achieves the true, valid relation to God and the world; and by this he becomes free from all bogging-down in the dead-ends of useless thoughts and illusory problems; free from one-sidedness, extravagance, self-illusion, repression, self-deceit and artificial evasion; he does not live in a world of subjective illusions. What a contrast to all extravagances, to all false spiritualism, is presented by the Liturgy! The prayers speak clearly and definitely of the frailty of man, the wretchedness of our souls and our misery. Nothing is idealistically embellished, nothing disavowed, neither our dependence nor our weakness and unreliableness. How classical is the Liturgy's attitude also toward the sphere of sex. It speaks quite openly of the birth of man in the *Ave Maria*, in the versicals after the prayer *Sacrosanctae* — *Beata viscera, quae portaverunt aeterni Patris Filium; Et beata ubera, quae lactaverunt Christum Dominum.* (Blessed the womb that bore Thee, and the paps which Thou hast sucked.)

What an inner liberty in the question of the Blessed Mary "How shall this be done because I know not man?", which figures in the Gospels of so many feasts dedicated to the Mother of God. What a grandiose audacity in the application of the Canticle of Canticles in the Liturgy! What a contrast to all prudishness, to the pretense that the sphere of sex does not exist and the hushing up still encountered in Catholic circles! What a spirit of truthfulness, a clear sight of all things *in conspectu Dei!* It is sufficient to recall the hymn in Compline and many other passages of the Liturgy.

On the other hand, we never find in the Liturgy

the disastrous, purely neutral treatment of the sphere of sex which is often met with today and is considered by many as a progress — that irreverent attitude which speaks of that sphere without any understanding of its character of mystery, the mysterious beauty which it possesses as a sphere of fulfillment of the highest union of love and its deepest symbolic expression. There is the same lack of understanding of the mystery of the coming into existence of a new human being, and of the *mysterium iniquitatis,* the mystery of sin implied in its abuse. Such an attitude is also typically unclassical. It is the result of the levelling, neutralizing, profoundly artificial attitude of the so-called new functionalism, which in reality is the most unobjective of all attitudes. There is nothing of that kind to be found in the Liturgy. This sphere is considered here in its two genuine aspects: as the danger-zone of sin, and a mysterious symbol of love and the birth of man as expressed in the application of the Canticle of Canticles in the Liturgy and in the rite of marriage.

In the Liturgy, we are not only enveloped in the classical, the genuine, in contrast with all extravagance and self-delusion, but we are also enveloped in the classical as the opposite of all one-sidedness. It is the classical character of the all-embracing, the totality of truth. The Liturgy breathes the air that is free from all local peculiarities, from all that is fortuitous and dependent on time. Above all it does not over emphasize *one* religious truth. It takes into account the multiple aspects of supernatural truth. In it there is no antithesis between the historical and pneumatic Christ; the mysterious unity of Christ the man and the eternal Logos clearly appears; it lets our eyes behold God's epiphany in the Son of the blessed Virgin, the incarnation of the blessed Word, at a definite historical moment, in a definite place, from the tribe of David.

In the numerous texts of the Gospel, which penetrate the entire Liturgy, in the feasts of the liturgical year, Christ's humanity unfolds before our eyes in its full concreteness and reality. In the epistles and readings of the Holy Sacrifice of the Mass, in the lessons of matins, in the psalms, in the action of the Sacrifice, in the beginning of St. John's Gospel, in the rites of the sacrament, the Messiah, the Mediator, the Saviour, the Logos made flesh, appears in His divine mystery. These two elements do not rise before us unlinked, juxtaposed, but in that ultimate reciprocal interpenetration corresponding to the two natures in one Person. Christ does not stand before us at one time as man and another time as God, but as the God-Man, as a man whose every word, every attitude, every act, and entire visible human being testifies to His divinity, and is an epiphany of God.

Today, one often opposes to a Christocentric piety in which Christ is adored as the God-Man, the theocentric piety in which through Christ and with Christ we adore the Father. In Christocentric piety, Christ so to speak stands before us and looks at us, while we at the same time look into His visage. In theocentric piety, Christ also stands before us, but He is turned towards the Father, on the summit of humanity so to speak, leading us to the Father and preceding us on that way. In Christocentric piety, we adore Christ. In theocentric piety, Christ is the mediator, the Head of humanity, our brother. Though the piety of certain ages, as for instance that of modern times, is often one-sided, Christocentrically directed, today the theocentric attitude is observed in opposition to the Christocentric one, and considered the only correct and genuinely Catholic one.

In reality, it is a mistake to oppose these two forms of relationship with Christ. Christ is both the eternal Word of the Father addressed to us, God's epiphany, and the Mediator between us and God, our Head through Whom alone we may adequately adore God. Christ eternally turns His visage both towards the Father *and* towards us. He is not only one who leads us to God like Moses; He not only stands at the side of humanity looking up at God together with humanity and leading it to God, but He also stands before us, as the self-revelation of God, as He who speaks to Philip: "Philip, he that seeth me, seeth the father also," and of whom St. John says: *Et vidimus Gloriam eius, gloria quasi unigeniti a patre, plenum gratiae et veritatis* (And we saw His glory, the glory as it were of the only begotten of the Father, full of grace and truth).

Our bond of union with Christ is not only a "we-communion," in which the exclusive Thou is God the Father; our bond of union is also an "I-and-thou communion." In the giving of ourselves by love to Christ, in becoming one with Him, we are drawn into the most Holy Trinity.

Though our we-communion with Christ, our membership in His Mystical Body is ontologically constituted in supernatural fashion through baptism. It would, nevertheless, remain dead without the giving of ourselves through faith and love to Christ. Thus especially the full transformation into Christ will never be achieved in us without the "I-thou" communion with Christ.

Once again we find in the Liturgy both these aspects in their mysterious interpenetration. In the Holy Mass, we sacrifice with Christ, our Head; He is turned toward the Father, and He does not turn away from the Father when in Holy Communion His visage is turned towards us, and through this communion of love with Him we are enfolded through His holy humanity into His Godhood. At Christmas, and especially on the feast of the Epiphany, Christ stands before us as the God become man, as the Word of the Father, which He addresses to us. The Christmas Preface expresses this with a particular clearness: *Quia per incarnati Verbi mysterium, nova mentis nostrae oculis lux tuae clari-*

tatis infulsit: ut dum visibiliter Deum cognoscimus,
per hunc in invisibilium amorem rapiamur. (For
by the mystery of the Word made flesh the light of
Thy glory hath shone anew upon the eyes of our
mind so that while we acknowledge Him as God seen
by man we may be drawn by Him to the love of
things unseen.)   In the orisons, Christ stands once
more as Mediator before us.   In the psalms also
we join in His prayer to the Father.   In certain
hymns, as in the *Jesu dulcis memoria,* the adoration
of Christ prevails.

Here these two aspects are not juxtaposed but organically interpenetrated, as especially in the Holy
Mass and Communion; they are indeed but two
aspects of one and the same mystery, the Incarnation.

Concerning the saints, these two aspects analogously are found in the Liturgy.   Sometimes we are
united with the saints in the great communion of
the Mystical Body of Christ and adoring with them;
we face God; at other times we lift our eyes from
the valley of tears to the Heavenly Jerusalem, and
we behold the saints reflecting Christ and manifesting God.   We see the saints as our intercessors, and

also as witnesses to the *magnalia Dei,* as a reflection of God's glory, as persons in whom Christ lives, who radiate Him and manifest God through Him.

Both aspects are of a classical nature. Both find their full expression in the liturgy. In the prayers of the Canon, *Communicantes* and the *Nobis quoque peccatoribus,* both aspects appear in their interpenetration. In the *Suscipe Sancte Pater* of the Offertory, the gaze lifted to the heavenly Jerusalem prevails. The fact that there are feasts dedicated to the saints, at which the Holy Mass is said in their honour, reflects once more the aspect of the Heavenly Jerusalem. This is the aspect reflected in the Introit of the feast of All Saints: *Gaudeamus omnes in Domino, diem festum celebrantes sub honore Sanctorum omnium* (Let us all rejoice in the Lord, celebrating a festival day in honour of all the saints). In the orisons of the Mass, on the contrary, in which we ask God to hearken to our prayers because of the saints' merits, we are again directed to the other aspect.

The classical element of the Liturgy is especially expressed in the totality of truth. The man formed by the Liturgy will not fall into the exaggeration and isolation of one truth only; he will not cling to one aspect only; he will live from an organic, synoptic vision and the entire plenitude of supernatural truth.

The Liturgy does not display one particular form of piety among many others. It is the piety of the Church itself, the praying Christ. Actually there is no specific liturgical piety; for Liturgy is the accomplishment of the Mystical Body of Christ itself, of true relationship with God. True mysticism and asceticism belong organically to the Liturgy as parts of the general relationship of man with God. They not only present no contradiction, but they flow moreover directly out of the liturgical act. Validly performed, the Liturgy naturally includes asceticism; it is sufficient to recall Lent, the Ember days, the Vigils, the immanent mortification involved in the proper physical comportment during prayer. And more so, the Liturgy performed with full consciousness includes meditation and contemplation. Let us recall Matins and its lessons. Indeed, those who really understand the spirit of the Liturgy will also understand the necessity of an explicit *inner prayer*, of the complete emptying of oneself before God, standing before Him, harkening, making room for

God in us, and letting God become the Word in us. They will know how difficult for our fallen nature is recollection, emerging from the tensions centered on the coming moment, restraining the impulse to rush toward that which comes next. They will become aware of the danger of drawing the liturgical act into the turmoil of activism, and accomplishing it as a mere duty. But the highest goal for the practise of inner prayer, namely walking before God, will reach its climax precisely in the entirely awake and ultimate participation in the Liturgy. Here also is to be found the primal source of all true mysticism, that is to say of the conscious, grace-inspired experience of the most Holy Trinity in us.

The organic matrix for all asceticism is the confrontation with God achieved in the Liturgy; and so too the mystery performed in the Liturgy is the organic primal basis of all mysticism. From the Liturgy everything receives its inner classical form. The asceticism and contemplation achieved fully in the Liturgy are the highest of all. It is not the ascetic aspect as such, nor the longing to touch and experience the Holy Trinity dwelling in us through baptism which prevail here as something isolated. It is mortification as a direct corollary to the life of Christ which is achieved in the Liturgy, and mysticism as the true *experience* of the mystery, if it is granted of course, as a free gift of God, which comes from participation in the glorification of God through Christ, with Christ and in Christ.

*   *

*

Should we not fall on our knees before God in adoring thanksgiving for the ineffable gift of the Liturgy when we consider the narrowness and limitation of man, and how easily even faithful Catholics moved by good-will slip away from the spirit of Christ; when we consider further how even when they do not sin, they make for themselves an image of Christ according to their own narrowness, reflect this falsified image, and mix up the various levels of depth within themselves; when we realize that only in the saint do we meet the true spirit of Christ and that only saints as for example Saint Paul, Saint Augustine, Saint Francis of Assisi and Saint Catherine of Siena radiate an unfalsified image of Christ;

— our gratitude should know no boundaries when we hear the priest pronounce the *Introibo ad altare Dei* and the Holy Sacrifice of Mass begins; when the *"Deus in adjutorium meum intende"* solemnly resounds at the beginning of the Divine Office; when we are enveloped in this ultimate, fully genuine world of truths; when we grasp that here, independently of our narrowness, errors and slumbers, God is adored in Truth and Spirit; that the true, genuine "Word" is spoken to God, because Christ Himself sacrifices, praises and glorifies God in our midst, and that *we* are allowed to become "true," that *we* are allowed to sacrifice to God, to adore and praise Him through Christ, with Christ and in Christ. Then an endless stream of gratitude surges up within us. Then we experience what the Church is, what the Mystical Body of Christ is, and that God loved us first, before we loved Him.

It seems inconceivable, then, that so many Catholics feed on stones instead of bread, lead a life in which their contact with this stream of divine life is so limited and so restricted to the mere duty of attending Holy Mass on Sundays. Others who attend Mass more frequently and receive Communion,

do not attain, in spite of this, a full conscious participation in the mystery, because they only "pray in
the Mass" and do not follow the recommendation of
the saintly Pope Pius X, to "pray the Mass."   They
do not know the Divine Office.   Even among priests
who are *obliged* to recite the Divine Office daily
there are some who do this only as another duty.
They are not aware that through the Divine Office
they are *allowed* to draw from the true sources of the
spirit of Christ.   Considering all this, we would like
to shout to all those who live in the House of God and
who do not yet know the *ubertas domus Domini* (the
plenitude of the fruitfulness of the House):

"O taste and see that the Lord is sweet." . . .
"With joy shall ye draw water out of the wells of the
Saviour and in that day shall ye say: Praise the
Lord and call upon His name" *"Gustate et videte,
quod suavis est Dominus."*. . . *"Haurietis aquas in
gaudio defontibus salvatoris et dicetis in die illa
confitemini Domino et invocate nomen eius."*